MARY BERRY FAST CAKES

Easy Bakes in Minutes

Quercus

Quercus
New York • London

First published by Quercus in the United States in 2019
First published as *Fast Cakes* and *More Fast Cakes* in 1981 and 1988 by Piatkus

ISBN 978-1-63506-126-0
eISBN 978-1-63506-127-7

Library of Congress Control Number: 2018956454

Commissioning editor: Muna Reyal
Project editor: Jo Roberts-Miller
Recipe consultant: Lucy Young
Design and art direction: Smith & Gilmour
Photography: Georgia Glynn Smith
Food styling: Lisa Harrison and Isla Murray
Food styling assistant: Evie Harbury
Prop styling: Olivia Wardle
Recipe testing: Lucinda McCord and Isla Murray

Distributed in the United States and Canada by
Hachette Book Group
1290 Avenue of the Americas
New York, NY 10104

Manufactured in China

10 9 8 7 6 5 4 3 2 1

www.quercus.com

CONTENTS

Many friends make cakes simply because they love baking—they enjoy making things with their children and grandchildren, and some friends just bake for special occasions—while other friends only bake under duress because they have promised in a moment of madness to provide something for a local fête or school bazaar. When I ask why so many people are put off by the idea of making cakes, "It's such a business!" they tell me. "All that creaming of butter and sugar. I never seem to have the butter soft enough. And then the tins have to be lined and everything has to be just so. It's all right for you," they add accusingly, "you enjoy it!"

Well, so I do. But they are quite wrong if they think that you have to take a whole day off in order to make cakes successfully. Cakes, tea breads and biscuits can all be made quickly and easily with the minimum of fuss and trouble. There is no need to bother with fancy tins or piping bags to produce an informal yet professional finish to all kinds of teatime specialities.

When I sat down to list the different varieties of bake that could conceivably be included in a book on Fast Cakes, I was amazed how quickly I covered the paper. In quite a short time I had written down well over 150 recipe suggestions. Many of them are easy enough even for keen children to make, and I always like to encourage them. Both boys and girls enjoy baking and are so proud when it comes to presenting the results. And among the recipes included here must be several dozen to tempt even the most reluctant cake maker!

If you are new to baking, take some time to go through the following pages before you get started. I have included lists of basic equipment, key ingredients for the store cupboard and tips on how to achieve a successful bake every time, among other useful bits and pieces of information. Whatever you do, though, try to have fun with your baking, and the end results will be even more enjoyable.

Mary Berry

BASIC EQUIPMENT

BAKING TINS (PANS)

The recipes in this book use one or other of the following tins:

- 7 in round sandwich tins
- 8 in round sandwich tins
- 7 in deep round cake tin
- 7 in shallow square cake tin
- 8 in deep cake tin—round and square
- 8 in loose-bottomed cake or springform tin
- 8 in loose-bottomed, deep, fluted tart tin
- 9 in deep round cake tin (for the Christmas cake)
- 10 in shallow ovenproof dish
- 9 x 5 in (2 lb) loaf tin
- 8½ x 4½ in (1 lb) loaf tin
- 11 x 7 in baking tin
- 12 x 9 in traybake (sheetcake) tin
- 13 x 9 in Swiss roll tin
- 3 in loose-bottomed fluted mini tart tins
- 2 shallow bun (muffin top) tins
- 1 deep, 12-hole muffin tin
- 2 large, heavy, flat baking sheets

ALL MEASUREMENTS GIVEN ARE THE INTERNAL DIMENSIONS You might find your traybake tin, for example, is listed as 13 x 9 in when the internal dimensions are in fact 12 x 9 in. Also, some loaf tins of the same capacity can be different shapes. We use the long variety, rather than the deeper ones that are also available. This won't impact any of the tea bread recipes, for example—your finished bake will just be a bit shorter and deeper than mine—but it may affect a recipe if the loaf tin is lined with one of the ingredients—see page 114 for Mocha Brandy Gâteau.

MARKING TIN SIZES AND CAPACITIES Scratch the diameter measurements on the bottom of cake tins and the sizes on the bottom of baking tins—it saves measuring every time. I also write the capacities on the base of porcelain and glass oven dishes with a freezer or ovenproof marker pen—this is such a help when it comes to making a flan and you wonder whether your dish will take a certain amount of liquid.

COOLING RACKS

When the cakes are cooked, they have to be cooled. It helps, therefore, to have:

- 2 large cooling racks—but you can, of course, always use the grid from your grill pan.

SMALL BAKE PAPER LINERS

Small bake paper liners do vary in size—some are called cupcake cases, others fairy cake cases or simply small cake cases. In order to get around this issue, a general rule to follow is that if you want to ice your small bakes with a glacé icing, make sure you only fill the cases to within ½ in from the top of the case. That way, even when the cakes rise there is still some of the edge of the paper liner above the cake. It is less important if the cakes are to be uniced, or if you are icing them with a buttercream. If you are making Butterfly Cakes (see page 168), however, it's important to fill the liners to just below the rim so that when they bake they rise above the paper liner and give you some cake to slice off and turn into butterfly wings.

For the purposes of our small bakes, we have used two different paper liners—muffin liners and tiny petit four cups.

Beware of cheap paper cases! Once baked, they come away from the fairy cake or muffin.

PREPARATION EQUIPMENT FOR A KEEN BAKER

- A selection of oven-safe ***glass mixing bowls*** that fit inside one another.
- ***2 plastic or rubber spatulas***—this cuts out waste, enabling you to get all the mixture off the sides of the bowls. It makes the children cross, however, because there is not enough mixture left in the bowl for them to lick!
- ***1 offset spatula*** for spreading icing and lifting biscuits off their baking sheets.
- ***1 long slotted spatula*** for lifting out slices of cake from roasting tins.
- ***1 cake spatula*** for moving cakes around safely.
- A set of ***measuring spoons*** for measuring ingredients such as baking powder or spices—they usually come as ¼ teaspoon, ½ teaspoon, 1 teaspoon and 1 tablespoon. All amounts given in the recipes are for level spoonfuls.
- ***1 wire balloon whisk*** for beating eggs or small amounts of cream. It gives a light mixture.
- ***1 wooden spatula or spoon***—I prefer using a spatula because it is flat on both sides and is easy to scrape clean.
- ***Nonstick baking paper*** for lining cake tins. Time-saving tip: use a spare moment to cut several circles to fit the tin you use most often and store them in a bag in a drawer, or buy them already cut.
- ***Long-life silicone mats*** is available in packets or on a roll. It is invaluable for lining the baking sheet when you make meringues or other sugary things as it really is nonstick. Best of all, it can be used time and time again. I just shake off the sugar, fold the paper and put it back in the packet for next time. You can draw circles on it to use as a guide when shaping meringue rings or pavlova, or buy them already cut.
- ***Food mixer***—I always use a mixer when making a cake with the all-in-one method. Whether you have a table model or a hand-held mixer, though, follow the instructions provided with your mixer.
- ***Food processor***—take care not to overmix! As with a food mixer, it is important to follow the instructions that come with the machine.

USEFUL STORAGE AIDS AND EQUIPMENT

- ***Plastic wrap*** is excellent for wrapping cakes because it keeps the moisture in. Its other great advantage is that you can see what it contains! It is also useful for lining tins when making refrigerator cakes—see No-Bake Chocolate Juliette on page 113.
- ***Paper towels***—how did we ever exist without paper towels? At one time, cloths and tea towels had to be used for covering and wrapping foods and these needed constant washing and drying so that they could be used again. Paper towels are useful for placing between layers of shortbreads, etc., in storage tins. It is absorbent and handy for wiping up spills as well.
- ***Airtight storage containers***—remember to store cakes and biscuits separately. If you put them together, the biscuits will go soft. Any tins that would rust are best kept in a dry, warm cupboard. Store cake tins one inside the other. Baking sheets and Swiss roll tins are best stored vertically between two divisions, as you would store tea trays.
- ***Polyethylene boxes*** with clips to close are useful in various sizes to fit cakes or bakes.

PREPARATION METHODS

All-in-one means exactly what it says. Everything goes into the same container at once—either into a bowl for mixing with an electric food mixer, or into a large saucepan for mixing by melting (for example, the Honey Cake on page 90). Apart from the speed of preparation, this also cuts down on the washing up.

Do follow the recipes carefully and use both self-raising flour and a little baking powder for the all-in-one method. Mixing in this way is far quicker than in traditional cake making, so there is not enough air beaten into the mixture to make it rise using flour alone. You need the baking powder to give the extra lift. But do stick to the amount of baking powder given in the recipe—if you use too much, the cake will rise quickly when it first goes into the oven and then flop down before it is fully cooked.

A food mixer is perfect for all-in-one mixtures—my own is in constant use—but do take care not to overmix. Check through your instruction book for any special tips. I often put more mixture than I really should into my free-standing mixer. I prevent the flour from showering all over the floor by carefully covering the front end of the machine and the bowl with a kitchen towel. If you do the same, remember to stand by the machine while it is mixing to be sure that the kitchen towel does not accidentally slip into the mixture and get caught up in the paddle!

HOW MUCH MIXTURE A CAKE TIN TAKES

- 2 x 7 in sandwich tins take 1 lb (450g) at 350°F/Convection 320°F and need about 25 to 30 minutes cooking time.
- 2 x 8 in sandwich tins take 1½ lb (675g) at 350°F/Convection 320°F and need about 35 minutes cooking time.
- 18 small cakes take 1 lb (450g) at 400°F/Confection 350°F and need about 15 minutes cooking time.
- 7 in round cake tin takes 2½ lb (1.1kg) at 320°F/Convection 270°F 3 for about 1½ hours for a fruit cake.
- 8 in round cake tin takes 3¾ lb (1.7kg) at 320°F/Convection 270°F and needs about 2½ hours for a fruit cake.
- 7 in square tin as for a 8 in round tin.

HOW MUCH MIXTURE A CAKE TIN TAKES WITH WHISKED CAKES

- 2 x 7 in sandwich tins take a 3-egg mix. Bake at 375°F/Convection 325°F for about 20 minutes.
- 2 x 8 in sandwich tins take a 4-egg mix. Bake at 375°F Convection 325°F 5 for about 25 minutes.
- 13 x 9 in Swiss roll tin takes a 3-egg mix. Bake at 425°F/Convection 375°F for about 10 minutes.

TIPS FOR SUCCESS EVERY TIME

1 ***Choose a recipe that is going to be popular with the family.*** If you know it is all going to be eaten on the day it is made you can choose one that wouldn't keep, such as Just Rock Cakes (see page 185) or Classic Special Scones (see page 298). If you want it to last for some time in the cake tin choose a rich one like the Vicarage Fruit Cake (see page 146). If you know that one of your family or friends loathes coconut, ginger or banana then obviously avoid these flavors! Of all the recipes I have included, some, I must admit, are more popular with my family than others. If it's any help to you, these are the ones we enjoy most and that have become my standbys:

FOR EVERYDAY

Just Rock Cakes
Mincemeat Cake
Fruit Malt Loaf
Classic Special Scones
Proper Shortbread
Fairings
Botermoppen
Easy Apple Cake
Lemon Drizzle Traybake

FOR SPECIAL OCCASIONS

Coffee Fudge Traybake
Superb Carrot Cake
Fresh Raspberry Cream Pavlova
Special Apricot Cake
Brandy Snaps
No-Bake Chocolate Juliette
Gingerbread
Summer Raspberry Shortbread
Victoriana Christmas Cake
Chocolate Éclairs

WITH CHILDREN IN MIND

Millionaire's Shortbread
Annabel's Caramel Bars
Caroline's Chocolate Slab
Sultana Flapjacks
Simple Chocolate Cake with Fudge Icing
Chocolate Cream Fingers
Iced Shape Biscuits

2 ***Check that you have time to make the recipe and bake it before starting.*** To help I have put the preparation and baking times. Remember, though, that your preparation time could be longer if you have to chop the almonds or defrost some cream from the freezer to fill a sponge. If you have to nip out and see a neighbor, select a recipe that uses the all-in-one method. The mixture can be prepared and put in the tins ready for baking when you return. They seem to rise just as well. The uncooked mixture will not spoil if, as so often happens with me, the ten minutes you thought you would be away turns into half an hour. Cakes already in the oven are not so accommodating!

I have found that you can split the preparation and baking of other recipes, such as fruit cakes, tea breads and shortbread type biscuits. Very often I prepare the mixture for all-in-one Victoria sandwiches and then find that I have an unexpectedly long phone call and there is no time to bake them before, say, fetching the children from school. I simply put the mixture in the tins and then bake them when I get back. Biscuits and shortbread can in fact improve by being left to chill in the fridge before baking. Recipes that you must prepare and then bake straightaway are whisked sponges, meringues and any recipes with beaten egg whites folded in at the end of the recipe.

3 ***Make sure you have everything you need before you start baking:*** the cake tin or tins and all the ingredients. And don't improvise with ingredients unless you've tried the recipe at least once before! Gather the ingredients together, weighing them carefully and ticking the items off in pencil, if you like. This way you won't forget to add the sugar! Time can be saved by weighing the ingredients straight into the mixing bowl. Incidentally, I have deliberately left salt out of most of the recipes. I find it makes no difference to the flavor and using it means one more thing to remember!

4 ***Make sure you read the recipe properly!*** It's very important to do this, even though you may feel you know the method.

5 ***Mixing the recipe.*** I have tried to use the all-in-one method whenever possible because it is fast and effective. Take a large roomy bowl, put in all the ingredients and beat with an electric mixer until well blended. I find it a marvellously sound way of mixing and I would never go back to the traditional method. If you prefer to use butter instead of margarine, then allow it to become soft and creamy before adding it. Take care not to get it too warm because the butter will be an oily consistency.

6 ***Follow the method conscientiously.*** I don't believe you will think of a short cut I haven't already tried! The method I give for each recipe is one that, from experience, I find works best. So, if you are the sort of person who likes to experiment, may I respectfully suggest you wait until you've had a go doing it my way first!

7 ***Mixing with an electric mixer saves considerable time.*** I use both a free-standing and a hand-held mixer constantly. If you're canny and plan a baking morning, you can start by rubbing in fat to flour for pastry, then make a plain cake then a chocolate cake without washing up the mixer in between! I find using an electric mixer best for all-in-one cakes. If using a free-standing mixer, beat for 1 minute or for a hand-held mixer 2 minutes. When adding dried fruit, it is often best to do this by hand or to just mix for a few seconds as the fruit could easily be chopped up, which would spoil the mixture. You can, of course, beat by hand but that will take a little longer. Food processors are marvelous for making pastry, chopping nuts and rubbing mixtures, too.

8 ***Prepare your tins.*** To save time in the long run, use nonstick paper or long-life silicone paper to line baking sheets. When biscuits are cooked, they slide off easily. With experience, you will soon find that sometimes you can just grease the baking sheet, for example when baking scones. You will know whether your own cake tins stick or not, but I prefer to buy loose-bottomed round cake and sandwich tins or to line an ordinary cake tin with nonstick baking paper. It is maddening to have a cake stick to a tin, so I consider it well worth bothering to take care and line them first. Be sure to prepare well the baking sheets for meringues and sugary items that really stick. I recommend lining the baking sheets with long-life silicone paper or nonstick baking paper.

9 ***The temperature of the oven is most important when baking.*** If you are not absolutely certain that your oven temperature is correct, beg, borrow or buy an oven thermometer and carry out a check yourself. Buying a thermometer is cheaper than asking a utility engineer to visit your home and test your thermostat. Alternatively, if in practice you notice that your cakes always take a longer or shorter time to cook than is given in the recipe, adjust the oven setting accordingly next time and make a note of it. And never open the oven door during the early part of the baking time or move the cake tin in the oven. Both actions will make the cake sink in the middle.

USING CONVENTIONAL GAS OR ELECTRIC OVEN If only one item is being baked, bake on the center shelf. If baking two, either put both on the same shelf or consult the manufacturers' manual as to shelf positions.

USING A CONVECTION OVEN The baking times and temperatures differ from the conventional ovens so do consult the manufacturers' manual and take their advice. Usually, you need to decrease the baking temperature by approximately 30°F. For example, something like a Victoria sandwich bakes at 350°F in a conventional oven and 320°F in a convection oven.

USING A MICROWAVE OVEN Consult the manufacturers' manual for baking methods and times. It is difficult to give advice generally as the electrical output of the different makes and models of microwaves varies. Microwave ovens certainly speed up the baking time but unless the cake is flavored with chocolate or coffee the appearance is a little pale and disappointing. However, this can be overcome by icing or frosting the cake. Cakes must be baked in nonmetallic containers.

BAKING SEVERAL CAKES IN ONE GO ON DIFFERENT SHELVES Even though modern ovens are thermostatically controlled, I find that if several items are baked at once they take longer to cook and in the case of a three-tier wedding cake it can lengthen the time by an hour or so. Keep an eye on them during the latter part of the baking and, lifting them carefully without banging, move the tins or baking sheets around so that each batch is evenly browned. Forgetful cooks would be well advised to use a pinger-timer to remind them to check. The timer, of course, should be set to go off at a shorter interval than the baking time in the recipe.

CHOOSING, USING AND STORING YOUR CAKE INGREDIENTS

Store your cake ingredients in a dry cupboard in logical sections, keeping the various flours, sugars and fruits together. Leave the flours in the bags they come in, and the sugars as well, unless you wish to decant the ones you use most, like superfine sugar. I also keep a separate jar of superfine sugar with added vanilla pods so that I always have vanilla sugar on hand for flavoring. If you buy goods in bulk, such as 7 lb (3kg) bags of dried fruit or large bags of flaked almonds, keep small amounts in the store cupboard and freeze the remainder in polyethylene bags for up to a couple of years.

FLOUR I always use a good-quality flour and in most cases the self-rising variety. Many of my recipes also use additional baking powder. Some recipes use whole-wheat or granary flour, but these usually replace only half of the white, so that the finished cake is not heavy (which would be the result of using all whole-wheat flour). Whole-wheat flour is more nutritious than white because it is less refined, and it gives us more fiber, which is recommended for good health. However, it does absorb more water or liquid than white flour, so more liquid is added in these recipes and extra baking powder is also added to make them rise sufficiently.

SUGAR In these recipes I have mostly used unrefined or natural sugars wherever possible. Unrefined demerara sugar is clearly labeled, and the muscovado sugars are both completely natural and have an excellent flavor. If necessary, light and dark soft brown sugars can be substituted for the respective muscovado sugars, but I find there is a loss of flavor.

It is essential to store all sugars in dry conditions, and confectioners' sugar should always be sifted before use. Remember when using golden syrup or molasses not to be overgenerous, as this can upset the balance of ingredients and alter the results of a recipe considerably.

EGGS All of the recipes use size 2 eggs (large 2 oz/50g), which give good results. I always find the best results are from eggs that have been left out of the fridge a little while before using them, so that they are at room temperature.

FATS AND OILS I prefer to use a high-fat baking spread/margarine instead of butter for most of my cakes. Spread for baking simplifies the making process because you do not have to remove it from the refrigerator and give it time to soften before you use it. In fact, it is important to use spread straight from the refrigerator. If it is too soft, the results are not as good. I use butter where the flavor is important, though, for example in Chewy Almond Flapjacks (see page 266) or in Traditional Dutch Butter Biscuits (see page 209), where the buttery flavor is essential. I use sunflower oil in recipes that need oil, as it is light and has a neutral flavor.

FRUIT It is not necessary to wash dried fruit now, as this is done before packaging and sale to the public. Always buy dried apricot pieces to use in a cake, as they will be cheaper than whole dried ones and it will also save the time that is taken up by chopping. Glacé cherries usually have a well of syrup in the center, so it is better to cut them in half or quarters and wash and dry them; this will prevent the fruit sinking in a cake.

SPICES It is important for ground spices to be kept dry and ideally in the dark, as they fade in sunlight. They should be replaced yearly as they tend to lose their flavor and potency.

NUTS If a recipe calls for chopped nuts, it is practical to buy broken or pieces of nut rather than whole ones: this not only saves money but time as well. Store nuts in separate bags for the different types in your freezer. In a store cupboard in a warm kitchen, nuts may go off quickly as the fat in them can turn rancid.

LEMONS I always use unwaxed lemons. If you use the waxed variety the zest will not have the best flavor. Warm lemons for a few minutes in a microwave to extract the maximum juice.

CHOCOLATE The strongest and most economical way of adding chocolate flavor is to use cocoa powder. If a recipe calls for melted chocolate, I have always used bittersweet or semisweet, as it is available at the grocery store.

COFFEE Coffee extract gives a good coffee flavor and, being a liquid, is easy to mix. However, if this is not available, instant coffee mixed with a little hot water and then added gives quite satisfactory results. Otherwise, you can use very strong proper coffee.

ONCE YOUR CAKE IS BAKED

HOW TO KNOW WHEN A CAKE IS DONE

There is no great mystery to baking a cake. It is done when it looks and smells ready. In most cases, the principal signs are when the cake shrinks slightly from the sides of the tin and when the top of the cake springs back after being pressed lightly with a finger.

Large fruit cakes need a further test. Simply push a fine metal skewer into the center of the cake and if it comes out clean and shiny, the cake is ready. If the skewer has some cake mixture clinging to it, cook for a few minutes longer, checking again from time to time. Sometimes, the cake is not quite done in the middle but the top is getting brown and the currants on the surface seem to be burning. In this case, place a piece of foil lightly on the top, lower the temperature and leave to cook for a bit longer.

HOW TO KNOW WHEN BISCUITS ARE DONE

With biscuits and shortbread, test by eye, checking that the color is right. As a general rule biscuits should be turning a gentle caramel brown color at the edges. Naturally chocolate-flavored items will be a darker color at the edges, not only on the top but underneath as well. It is sometimes difficult to tell when a thick shortbread is ready just by looking at the top, so I take the tin from the oven and lift a slice carefully out from the center. The underneath should be very pale golden brown and the middle of the underside should look short and cooked, not close and soggy.

Biscuits on the outside of the sheet may bake more quickly than those in the middle. In this case, transfer them to a wire rack and return the rest to the oven for a few more minutes.

COOLING BISCUITS

Remove from the oven, leave on the baking sheet to firm a little then slip an offset spatula under them and transfer to cool on a wire rack.

Store in an airtight container with wax paper between the layers.

COOLING CAKES

Leave cakes in the tin to cool for a while before turning them out on to a wire rack (10 minutes for a sponge sandwich, 30 minutes for a large cake, or see individual recipes). In order to turn the cake out quickly without breaking it, run a knife around the edge of the tin before inverting the tin. If the tin has been lined, turn upside down on to a folded kitchen towel, take away the tin, peel off the paper and transfer the cake to the cooling rack.

With all-in-one Victoria sandwiches, I turn out the sponges onto a wire rack and then replace the tins over them. This prevents the moisture from evaporating while the cakes are cooling and it does not make the sponges soggy.

Store cakes in an airtight container once cool.

FREEZING BISCUITS

There is little point in freezing biscuits as most of them keep for a couple of weeks in a container. However, they can be stored in the freezer for up to 3 months if required.

Raw shortbread type of biscuits can be rolled into sausage shapes, covered in plastic wrap and frozen. When slightly thawed, slices can be cut from the sausages and baked freshly as needed.

Incidentally, there is no need to freeze meringues, but you can if you wish.

FREEZING CAKES

All cakes freeze extremely well, except for those containing breakfast cereal, like cornflakes or Rice Krispies. Freeze them as soon as they are cool. If not iced or frosted, wrap them carefully in plastic wrap or put in a polyethylene box. If iced or frosted, freeze uncovered until solid then wrap carefully and label and return to the freezer to freeze solid. I try not to keep cakes in the freezer longer than three months, as those kept longer seem to lose a little of their flavor.

Fruit cakes and shortbreads, however, can stay in the freezer for many months, where I find they mature well. You may well ask why bother to freeze them at all, as they keep well in an airtight container in a cool, dry storage cupboard. Well, frankly, most kitchens are too warm for ideal storage conditions and some have insufficient room.

The freezer not only maintains the cakes in good condition, but it is also a deterrent to thieving fingers! The family is unlikely to raid the freezer, but a cake on the countertop is an open invitation!

HELP! IT HAS ALL GONE WRONG

Frankly, I don't think anything should go wrong but just in case you do have the occasional failure, here is a guide to the possible reasons:

ALL-IN-ONE MIXTURES

Coarse texture	Too much baking powder
Collar edge on cake	Rising of cake was too rapid and it then sank. One of two causes: either the cake was placed on too high a shelf in the oven, or there was too much baking powder in the mixture
Damp, close texture	Cake was removed from the oven too soon
Domed, cracked top	Oven too hot or cake placed too high in oven
Hollow top	Mixture beaten too long; too slow an oven; cooking time too short; spread for baking allowed to become oily during very hot weather
Pale in color although fully cooked	Oven too cool or cake placed on too low a shelf

MELTED MIXTURES

Cracked top	Too much baking powder, syrup or molasses, too hot an oven, door opened too early
Doughy texture	Too much flour or baking powder, not enough liquid
Hard on outside	Too much liquid or syrup; oven too hot

WHISKED MIXTURES

Specks of uncooked flour	Poor whisking; flour not mixed in properly
Sticky, damp texture when cold, sticking to sides of tin	Usually caused by being in too much of a hurry and skimping each stage; ingredients not correctly measured; underwhisking so the sugar has not properly dissolved; underbaking; tin badly prepared. Any or all of these will give sticky results
Too shallow, not risen	Insufficient whisking; too cool an oven; not enough baking powder
Uneven rising	Flour not folded in properly; oven shelves not level; mixture unevenly distributed in the tin before baking
Wrinkled top to cake	Underbaking; tin too small

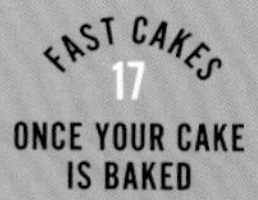

CHAPTER ONE

EVERYDAY CAKES

MAKING TIME 5 MINUTES
BAKING TIME 25–30 MINUTES

ALL-IN-ONE VICTORIA SANDWICH

I no longer prepare a Victoria sandwich with the traditional creaming and folding methods, as this all-in-one method gives excellent results every time. Make sure to use the margarine straight from the fridge—you don't want it too soft.

SERVES 8

- 1 cup (8 oz/225g) margarine, from fridge
- 1 cup (8 oz/225g) superfine sugar, plus extra to sprinkle
- 4 large eggs
- 2 cups (8 oz/225g) self-rising flour
- 1 level tsp baking powder
- 1 cup (8 oz/240ml) heavy cream
- 6–8 tbsp strawberry jam

1 Preheat the oven to 350°F/Convection 320°F. Grease two 8 in round sandwich tins and line the bases with nonstick baking paper.

2 Measure the margarine, sugar, eggs, flour and baking powder into a large mixing bowl and beat with an electric mixer until well blended and smooth.

3 Divide the mixture between the tins, level out evenly and bake in the preheated oven for 25–30 minutes, or until well risen and the tops of the sponges spring back when lightly pressed with a finger.

4 Leave to cool in the tins for a few minutes, then turn out, remove the paper and finish cooling on a wire rack.

5 To make the filling, measure the cream into a large bowl and whisk until stiff.

6 When completely cold, sandwich the cakes together with the jam and cream. Lift onto a serving plate and sprinkle with sugar.

MAKING TIME 5 MINUTES
BAKING TIME 25–30 MINUTES

LEMON SPONGE SANDWICH

If you can find orange curd, you could make this sponge sandwich with orange zest in place of the lemon and use orange curd as the filling.

SERVES 8

- 1 cup (8 oz/225g) margarine, from fridge
- 1 cup (8 oz/225g) superfine sugar, plus extra to sprinkle
- 4 large eggs
- 2 cups (8 oz/225g) self-rising flour
- 1 level tsp baking powder
- finely grated zest of 1 lemon
- about 6 tbsp lemon curd

1 Preheat the oven to 350°F/Convection 320°F. Grease two 8 in round sandwich tins and line the bases with nonstick baking paper.

2 Measure the margarine, sugar, eggs, flour, baking powder and lemon zest into a large mixing bowl and beat with an electric mixer until well blended and smooth.

3 Divide the mixture between the tins, level out evenly and bake in the preheated oven for 25–30 minutes, or until well risen and the tops of the sponges spring back when lightly pressed with a finger.

4 Leave to cool in the tins for a few minutes, then turn out, remove the paper and finish cooling on a wire rack.

5 When completely cold, sandwich the cakes together with the curd. Lift onto a serving plate and sprinkle with sugar.

MAKING TIME 5 MINUTES
BAKING TIME 25–30 MINUTES

COFFEE SPONGE SANDWICH

A lovely change to a classic Victoria sponge.

SERVES 8

2 heaped tsp instant coffee granules
1 cup (8 oz/225g) margarine, from fridge
1 cup (8 oz/225g) superfine sugar
2 cups (8 oz/225g) self-rising flour
4 large eggs
1 level tsp baking powder

For the icing

6 tbsp (3 oz/85g) butter, softened
2 cups (8 oz/225g) confectioners' sugar, sifted, plus extra to dredge
1 tbsp coffee extract

1 Preheat the oven to 350°F/Convection 320°F. Grease two 8 in round sandwich tins and line the bases with nonstick baking paper.

2 Dissolve the instant coffee in 1 tablespoon of boiling water and mix until smooth.

3 Measure the margarine, sugar, flour, eggs and baking powder into a large mixing bowl. Add the coffee mixture and beat with an electric mixer until well blended and smooth.

4 Divide the mixture between the tins, level out evenly and bake in the preheated oven for 25–30 minutes, or until well risen and the tops of the sponges spring back when lightly pressed with a finger.

5 Leave to cool in the tins for a few minutes, then turn out, remove the paper and finish cooling on a wire rack.

6 To make the icing, blend the butter with the confectioners' sugar and coffee extract.

7 When the cakes are completely cold, sandwich them together with the icing and lift onto a serving plate. Dredge with a little confectioners' sugar before serving.

MAKING TIME 15 MINUTES
BAKING TIME 55–60 MINUTES

MADEIRA CAKE

A classic cake.

SERVES 6

2 cups (8 oz/225g) self-rising flour
12 tbsp (6 oz/170g) butter, softened
¾ cup (6 oz/175g) superfine sugar
finely grated zest of 1 lemon
2 oz (50g) almond flour
4 large eggs
3 slices candied citron peel, to garnish (optional)

1 Preheat the oven to 350°F/Convection 320°F. Grease a deep, 7 in cake tin and line the base with nonstick baking paper.

2 Measure all the ingredients into a large mixing bowl and beat with an electric mixer until well blended and smooth.

3 Turn the mixture into the tin, level the top and bake in the preheated oven for 55–60 minutes. A skewer inserted into the center of the cake should come out clean. If desired, place 3 slices of citron peel on top of the cake after the first 30 minutes of cooking time.

4 Leave to cool in the tin for 15 minutes, then turn out and finish cooling on a wire rack.

5 Store in an airtight container.

MAKING TIME 20 MINUTES
BAKING TIME 25–30 MINUTES

COFFEE WALNUT GÂTEAU

If there is a lot left over, store slices in the freezer for up to 3 months.

SERVES 8

- 1 level tbsp instant coffee granules
- 12 tbsp (6 oz/170g) margarine, from fridge
- 1½ cups (4 oz/175g) superfine sugar
- 3 large eggs
- 1½ cups (4 oz/175g) self-rising flour
- 1 level tsp baking powder
- 2 oz (50g) walnuts, chopped

For the icing

- 6 tbsp (3 oz/85g) butter, softened
- 2 cups (8 oz/225g) confectioners' sugar, sifted
- 1 tbsp milk
- 1 tbsp coffee extract

For the decoration

- 10 walnut halves

1 Preheat the oven to 350°F/Convection 320°F. Grease two 8 in round sandwich tins and line the bases with nonstick baking paper.

2 Dissolve the instant coffee in 1 tablespoon of boiling water and mix until smooth.

3 Measure all the ingredients for the cake into a large mixing bowl and beat with an electric mixer until well blended and smooth.

4 Divide the mixture between the tins, level out evenly and bake in the preheated oven for 25–30 minutes, or until well risen and the tops of the cakes spring back when lightly pressed with a finger.

5 Leave to cool in the tins for about 5 minutes then turn out, remove the paper and finish cooling on a wire rack.

6 To make the icing, cream the butter and confectioners' sugar until smooth, then stir in the milk and coffee extract.

7 Sandwich the two cakes together with one-third of the icing. Spread the remainder over the top and sides of the cake and decorate with the walnut halves.

MAKING TIME 10 MINUTES
BAKING TIME 40–45 MINUTES

MARBLE CAKE

Children love this cake and it is not difficult to make and looks good when cut. Ice it as you like—try the chocolate icing on page 96—or serve it plain, sprinkled with confectioners' or superfine sugar.

SERVES 8

- 12 tbsp (6 oz/170g) margarine, from fridge
- 1½ cups (6 oz/175g) superfine sugar
- 1½ cups (6 oz/175g) self-rising flour
- 1 level tsp baking powder
- 3 large eggs
- 1 level tbsp cocoa powder
- 1 tbsp hot water
- a few drops red food coloring

1 Preheat the oven to 350°F/Convection 320°F. Grease a deep, 8 in cake tin and line with nonstick baking paper.

2 Measure the margarine, sugar, flour, baking powder and eggs into a large mixing bowl and beat with an electric mixer until well blended and smooth.

3 Measure the cocoa into another bowl with the water and stir thoroughly until blended and smooth. Add a third of the sponge mixture to this and mix together.

4 Put half of the remaining sponge mixture into a third bowl and color it pink with the food coloring.

5 Choose one of the mixtures and place tablespoons of this at regular intervals around the tin. Fill the gaps with the two other contrasting colors until all the mixture has been used. The cake will find its own level as it bakes so there is no need to smooth the top. Bake in the preheated oven for 40–45 minutes, or until golden brown, well risen and the top of the sponge springs back when lightly pressed with a finger.

6 Turn out and leave to cool on a wire rack. Ice or decorate as desired.

MAKING TIME 20 MINUTES
BAKING TIME 20–25 MINUTES

FRESH CREAM SPONGE CAKE

This sponge cake—topped with sprigs of mint and a few pretty flowerheads—is perfect to serve in the summer for tea. If you like, mix ½ cup fresh raspberries with the cream for a real treat. The sponge bases freeze well and can be frozen ahead then brought out of the freezer, thawed and filled when required.

SERVES 8

4 large eggs
1 cup (4 oz/100g) superfine sugar
1 cup (4 oz/100g) self-rising flour

For the filling

6–8 tbsp raspberry jam
1¼ cups (10 oz/300ml) heavy cream, whipped
½ cup (4 oz/100g) fresh raspberries, hulled

For the decoration

a little sifted confectioners' sugar
a sprig of fresh mint
small edible flowerheads (optional)

1 Preheat the oven to 350°F/Convection 320°F. Grease two 8 in round sandwich tins and line with nonstick baking paper.

2 Break the eggs into a warmed bowl and whisk in the sugar until the mixture is light and creamy and leaves a trail when the whisk is lifted out.

3 Sift in the flour and very carefully fold it in with a metal spoon.

4 Divide the mixture between the tins, level out evenly and bake in the preheated oven for 20–25 minutes, or until well risen and the tops of the sponges spring back when lightly pressed with a finger.

5 Turn out and leave to cool on a wire rack.

6 Spread one half of the cake with raspberry jam. Top with the whipped cream and scatter with the fresh raspberries. Sandwich the other cake on top, dust lightly with confectioners' sugar and decorate with a sprig of fresh mint and flowerheads, if desired, to serve.

MAKING TIME 15 MINUTES
BAKING TIME 20 MINUTES

SPECIAL LEMON CAKE

The lemon cream filling makes this sponge really rather special. It is at its best if you use homemade lemon curd. This is a fatless sponge, but the cream makes it extra special.

SERVES 8

- 4 large eggs
- ½ cup (4 oz/100g) superfine sugar
- 1 cup (4 oz/100g) self-rising flour
- ¾ cup (6 oz/180ml) heavy cream
- 6 tbsp good-quality lemon curd
- a little sifted confectioners' sugar

1 Preheat the oven to 375°F/Convection 325°F. Grease two 8 in round sandwich tins and line the bases with nonstick baking paper.

2 Put the eggs and sugar in a large heatproof bowl over a pan of lightly simmering water and whisk until the mixture is thick, white and creamy and leaves a thick trail when the whisk is lifted from the mixture. Remove from the heat and whisk for 2 minutes more.

3 Sift in the flour and very carefully fold it in with a metal spoon.

4 Divide the mixture between the tins, level out evenly and bake in the preheated oven for 20 minutes, or until well risen and the tops of the sponges spring back when lightly pressed with a finger.

5 Turn out onto a wire rack, remove the paper and leave to cool.

6 To make the filling, whisk the cream until thick, then fold in the lemon curd.

7 Sandwich the cakes together with the lemon cream and dust the top with confectioners' sugar before serving.

MAKING TIME 25 MINUTES
BAKING TIME 45–55 MINUTES

HONEY AND ALMOND CAKE

The sort of special cake that is just right for when Granny comes to tea. Because this basic cake mixture is not rich, it is best to make the base on the day or day before it is needed.

SERVES 6

- 10 tbsp (5 oz/140g) margarine, from fridge
- ½ cup (4 oz/100g) light muscovado sugar
- 2 tbsp runny honey
- 3 large eggs
- 1¼ cups (5 oz/150g) self-rising flour
- ¾ cup (2 oz/50g) almond flour
- 2 tbsp milk
- 1 tsp almond extract

For the filling and topping

- ½ cup (4 oz/114g) butter, softened
- 2 tbsp runny honey
- ½ tsp almond extract
- 1¼ cups (50 oz/150g) confectioners' sugar, sifted
- ¼ cup (2 oz/50g) slivered almonds, toasted

1 Preheat the oven to 320°F/Convection 270°F. Grease a deep, 7 in cake tin and line the base with nonstick baking paper.

2 Measure all the ingredients for the cake into a large mixing bowl and beat with an electric mixer until well blended and smooth.

3 Turn the mixture into the tin, level the top and bake in the preheated oven for 45–55 minutes, or until well risen and the tops of the cakes spring back when lightly pressed with a finger.

4 Leave to cool in the tin for about 10 minutes then turn out, remove the paper and finish cooling on a wire rack.

5 To make the filling and topping, measure the butter, honey, almond extract and confectioners' sugar into a bowl and mix well until thoroughly blended.

6 Slice the cake in half horizontally and sandwich together with half of the icing. Coat the sides of the cake with half of the remaining icing and roll in the toasted almonds so that the sides are evenly coated. Use the remaining icing to cover the top of the cake then sprinkle with the remaining almonds.

MAKING TIME 20 MINUTES
BAKING TIME 20–25 MINUTES

CLASSIC GENOESE

Best filled with whipped cream and soft fruit.

SERVES 6

3 large eggs
scant ½ cup (3½ oz/90g) superfine sugar
¾ cup (3½ oz/90g) self-rising flour
3 tbsp (1½ oz/40g) butter, melted and cooled

For the filling

⅔ cup (5 oz/150ml) heavy cream
about ½ cup (4 oz/100g) raspberries or sliced strawberries
about 1 level tbsp superfine sugar

1 Preheat the oven to 350°F/Convection 320°F. Grease two 7 in round sandwich tins and line the bases with nonstick baking paper.

2 Put the eggs and sugar in a heatproof bowl over a pan of hot water and whisk until the mixture is thick, white and creamy and leaves a trail when the whisk is lifted out of the bowl. Remove from the heat and whisk for 2 minutes more.

3 Sift the flour and carefully fold it into the mixture with a metal spoon.

4 Drizzle the butter around the edge of the mixture and carefully fold it in until it is evenly blended.

5 Divide the mixture between the tins, level out evenly and bake in the preheated oven for 20–25 minutes, or until golden brown, well risen and the tops of the sponges spring back when lightly pressed with a finger.

6 Turn out and leave to cool on a wire rack.

7 To make the filling, whisk the cream until it is thick and the mixture forms peaks. Fold in the fruit and sugar to taste.

8 When the cakes are cold, sandwich them together with the cream and fruit mixture.

MAKING TIME 15 MINUTES
BAKING TIME 1¼ HOURS

SPICY GINGER CAKE

This is a good basic ginger cake that will keep very well in an airtight container; in fact, it is better to keep it for three or four days before cutting.

MAKES 16 SQUARES

- ½ cup (4 oz/114g) margarine, from fridge
- ¾ cup (6 oz/175g) golden syrup (available online)
- ¼ cup (2 oz/50g) black molasses
- ¼ cup (2 oz/50g) dark brown sugar
- ⅔ cup (5 oz/150ml) milk
- 2 large eggs
- 2 cups (2 oz/225g) all-purpose flour
- 2 level tsp pumpkin pie spice
- 1 level tsp baking soda
- 2 level tsp ground ginger

1 Preheat the oven to 320°F/Convection 270°F. Grease an 8 in square cake tin and line with nonstick baking paper.

2 Measure the margarine, syrup, molasses and sugar into a small saucepan and heat gently until the margarine has melted.

3 Remove from the heat, add the milk and leave on one side to cool.

4 Beat the eggs then stir them into the cooled mixture.

5 Sift the flour into a bowl, together with the spice, baking soda and ginger. Make a well in the center and stir in the cooled milk and molasses mixture until well blended and smooth.

6 Pour into the tin and bake in the preheated oven for about 1¼ hours, or until risen and golden brown.

7 Turn out and leave to cool on a wire rack.

8 Cut into 16 squares and store in an airtight container.

MAKING TIME 15 MINUTES
BAKING TIME 10 MINUTES

SWISS ROLL

Homemade Swiss roll is not difficult if you follow these instructions and if you weigh all the ingredients accurately.

SERVES 8

4 large eggs, at room temperature
½ cup (4 oz/100g) superfine sugar, warmed
1 cup (4 oz/100g) self-rising flour

For the filling

superfine sugar, to sprinkle
about 5 tbsp raspberry jam

1 Preheat the oven to 425°F/Convection 375°F. Grease a 13 x 9 in Swiss roll tin and line with nonstick baking paper.

2 Whisk the eggs and sugar together in a large bowl until the mixture is light and creamy and the whisk leaves a trail when lifted out.

3 Sift the flour into the mixture and carefully fold it in with a metal spoon.

4 Turn the mixture into the tin and give it a gentle shake so the mixture finds its own level, making sure that it spreads evenly into the corners. Bake in the preheated oven for about 10 minutes, or until the sponge is golden brown and begins to shrink from the edges of the tin.

5 While the cake is baking, cut a piece of nonstick baking paper a little bigger than the tin and sprinkle it with sugar.

6 Remove the cake from the oven and invert onto the sugared paper. Quickly loosen the paper from the bottom of the cake and peel it off. To make rolling easier, make a score mark 1 in from one of the short edges, being careful not to cut through. Fold the narrow strip created by the score mark down and begin rolling, using the paper to keep a firm roll. Leave for a few minutes with the paper still around it so it will settle. Lift onto a wire rack.

7 When cool, remove the paper and spread the cake with jam, taking it almost to the edges. Reroll and sprinkle with more sugar before serving.

MAKING TIME 10 MINUTES
BAKING TIME 1¼ HOURS

SUPERB CARROT CAKE

This is a wonderfully gooey version. You could decorate it with walnut halves, if desired. I've added a small bake variation—these are easier for packed lunches, quicker to bake but equally delicious.

SERVES 12

- 2 cups (8 oz/225g) self-rising flour
- 1 level tsp baking powder
- ¾ cup (5 oz/150g) light muscovado sugar
- ¼ cup (2 oz/50g) walnuts, chopped
- 4 oz (100g) carrots, washed, trimmed and coarsely grated
- 2 ripe bananas, mashed
- 2 large eggs
- ½ cup (4 oz/150ml) sunflower oil

For the topping

- 4 tbsp (2 oz/55g) butter, softened
- 2 oz (50g) full-fat cream cheese
- 1¼ cups (5 oz/150g) confectioners' sugar, sifted
- ½ tsp vanilla extract

1 Preheat the oven to 350°F/Convection 320°F. Grease a deep, 8 in cake tin and line the base with nonstick baking paper.

2 Sift together the flour and baking powder into a large bowl and stir in the sugar. Add the nuts, carrots and bananas and mix lightly.

3 Make a well in the center, add the eggs and oil and beat until well blended.

4 Turn the mixture into the tin and bake in the preheated oven for about 1¼ hours, or until golden brown and shrinking slightly from the sides of the tin. A skewer inserted into the center of the cake should come out clean.

5 Turn out, remove the paper and leave to cool on a wire rack.

6 To make the topping, place all the ingredients in a bowl and beat with an electric mixer until well blended and smooth. Spread over the cake and rough up with a fork. Leave in a cool place to harden slightly before serving.

VARIATION: MINI CARROT CAKES

Prepare the cake mix as above and use to fill 12 paper liners set in a muffin tin. Bake for 25–30 minutes, until well risen and lightly brown. Prepare the topping as above and, once the cakes have cooled, use to top each cake.

MAKING TIME 30 MINUTES
BAKING TIME 35–40 MINUTES

BATTENBURG CAKE

This may not be as "fast" as some of the other cakes in the book, but it is such a family favorite that we felt it was important to include it. If you have a special 7 in Battenburg tin with divisions then do use it, but I've included here instructions on how to make your own divisions in a square tin.

SERVES 8

- ½ cup (4 oz/114g) margarine, from fridge
- ½ cup (4 oz/100g) superfine sugar
- 2 large eggs
- 1 cup (4 oz/100g) self-rising flour
- ½ level tsp baking powder
- ¼ cup (2 oz/50g) almonds flour
- 1 tsp vanilla extract
- 3 tsp milk
- a few drops red food coloring
- 8 oz (225g) marzipan

For the icing

- 1 cup (4 oz/100g) confectioners' sugar, plus extra to dust
- 3 tbsp (1½ oz/40g) butter, softened
- 1 tsp vanilla extract
- a few drops milk, if needed

1 Preheat the oven to 320°F/Convection 270°F. Grease a 7 in square cake tin. Cut out a piece of parchment-lined foil or baking paper that is 3 in longer than one side of the tin. Fold the paper in half widthwise with the foil-side on the inside. Open out the paper and push up the center fold to make a 1½ in pleat. Line the base of the tin with this, foil-side down, making any adjustments to ensure the pleat runs down the center of the tin.

2 Measure the margarine, sugar, eggs, flour, baking powder and almond flour into a large bowl and beat with a wooden spoon for 2–3 minutes until smooth, slightly lighter in color and glossy looking.

3 Spoon just very slightly more than half the mixture into a separate bowl and stir in the vanilla extract and 1½ teaspoons of the milk. Set aside.

4 Mix the food coloring with the remaining 1½ teaspoons of milk, then stir this into the other bowl of mixture.

5 Spoon the vanilla mixture into one half of the tin and the pink mixture into the other half. Level the surface of each half with a knife. Check the paper divider is still straight and in the middle.

6 Bake in the center of the preheated oven for 35–40 minutes, or until well risen and shrinking slightly from the sides of the tin.

RECIPE CONTINUES

7 Leave to cool in the tin for a few minutes then turn out, remove the paper and finish cooling on a wire rack.

8 To make the icing, sift the confectioners' sugar into a medium bowl and measure in the butter and the vanilla extract. Beat everything together with a wooden spoon until soft and smooth. Add a few drops of milk if the icing is a bit stiff.

9 Trim the crispy outer edges off the cooled cake with a serrated knife, then cut and trim, if necessary, into 4 equal lengthways strips—you need 2 vanilla and 2 pink strips. Lay 1 vanilla and 1 pink strip side by side, then use a little of the butter icing to stick them together. Spread a bit more icing on top. Stick the remaining 2 strips together with icing and lay these on top of the bottom cakes so when the 4 are put together they create a checkerboard effect. Cut two pieces of string, one that is the length of the assembled cake and one that will wrap all around it, in order to help you roll the marzipan to the correct size. Finally, spread a bit more icing over the top of the assembled checkerboard.

10 Lightly dust a work surface with sifted confectioners' sugar and roll out the marzipan into an oblong the length of the cake and sufficiently wide to wrap around the cake, using the pieces of string as your measuring guide. Lay the iced side of the cake onto the marzipan, positioning it so when you lift up one long side, it perfectly covers one side of the cake (this way the join will be neatly in the corner). Spread the rest of the icing over the remaining 3 sides of the cake (not the ends). Brush off any crumbs from the marzipan and work surface so they don't stick. Roll the cake over in the marzipan, pressing to neatly cover it, then brush the corner join lightly with water, pressing it to seal. (Try to avoid touching the marzipan with wet fingers as it will mark.) Turn the cake over so the join is on the bottom. Trim a slim slice from each end of the cake to neaten and show off the checkerboard effect. Smooth the marzipan with your hands so their warmth will give it a smooth finish.

MAKING TIME 10 MINUTES
CHILLING TIME 30 MINUTES
BAKING TIME 25–30 MINUTES

SHOOFLY PIE

This rather sweet pie is a traditional Pennsylvania Dutch dessert and is a perennial favorite. Serve it cut into wedges when you are looking for something different to offer at your coffee morning. The pastry must be thin in order for it to cook without blind baking.

SERVES 8

For the shortcrust pastry
1¼ cups (6 oz/175g) all-purpose flour
1 level tbsp confectioners' sugar
6 tbsp (3 oz/85g) butter, cubed
1 large egg, beaten
about 1 tbsp cold water

For the filling
½ cup (4 oz/100g) seedless raisins
¼ cup (2 oz/50g) light or dark muscovado sugar
3 tbsp hot water
¼ level tsp baking soda

For the topping
1 cup (4 oz/100g) all-purpose flour
½ level tsp ground cinnamon
¼ level tsp ground ginger
¼ level tsp ground nutmeg
4 tbsp (2 oz/55g) unsalted butter
¼ cup (2 oz/50g) light or dark muscovado sugar

1 You will need a deep, 8 in loose-bottomed, fluted tart tin.

2 To make the pastry, measure the flour, confectioners' sugar and butter into a food processor. Whizz until breadcrumb stage. Add the egg and water and whizz again until a dough is formed. Roll out thinly on a floured work surface and use to line the tin. Prick the base and sides all over with a fork and leave to chill in the fridge for 30 minutes.

3 Preheat the oven to 375°F/Convection 325°F and put a heavy baking sheet in the oven on the shelf just above the center.

4 To make the topping, sift the flour and spices together into a bowl and rub in the butter until the mixture resembles fine breadcrumbs. Carefully stir in the sugar.

5 Remove the pastry from the fridge and cover with the raisins. Mix the sugar with the hot water and baking soda and pour over the raisins.

6 Sprinkle the topping over the raisins, then place on the baking sheet in the preheated oven and bake for 25–30 minutes, or until golden brown.

7 Leave to cool in the tin, then lift out onto a serving plate. Serve cut into wedges.

MAKING TIME 15 MINUTES
CHILLING TIME 30 MINUTES
BAKING TIME 30 MINUTES

MINCEMEAT AND ALMOND TART

Serve either warm or cold. A rather different way of serving this traditional tart, the mincemeat complements the almond flavor well.

SERVES 8

For the shortcrust pastry
1¼ cups (6 oz/175g) all-purpose flour
1 level tbsp confectioners' sugar
6 tbsp (3 oz/85g) butter, cubed
1 large egg
about 1 tbsp cold water

For the filling
½ cup (4 oz/114g) butter
½ cup (4 oz/100g) superfine sugar
2 large eggs, beaten
1 cup plus 1 tbsp (4 oz/100g) almond flour
1 tsp almond extract
4 heaping tbsp mincemeat

1 You will need a deep, 8 in loose-bottomed, fluted tart tin.

2 To make the pastry, measure the flour, confectioners' sugar and butter into a food processor. Whizz until breadcrumb stage. Add the egg and water and whizz again, until a dough is formed. Roll out thinly on a floured work surface. Line the tin and prick the base and sides. Leave to chill in the fridge for 30 minutes.

3 Preheat the oven to 400°F/Convection 350°F.

4 To make the filling, heat the butter in a small pan until it has just melted. Stir in the sugar, beaten egg, ground almonds and almond extract.

5 Spread the mincemeat over the base of the crust, then spread the buttery filling on top. Bake in the preheated oven for about 30 minutes, or until golden brown and the filling springs back when lightly pressed with a finger.

6 Leave to cool on a wire rack, then lift out onto a serving plate. Serve cut into wedges.

MAKING TIME 15 MINUTES
CHILLING TIME 30 MINUTES
BAKING TIME 35 MINUTES

ALMOND BAKEWELL TART

This makes a delicious tart and, if you like, you could make the mixture as small individual tarts, but this will, of course, take longer. The pastry must be thin in order for it to cook without blind baking.

SERVES 8

For the shortcrust pastry

1¼ cups (6 oz/175g) all-purpose flour
1 level tbsp confectioners' sugar
6 tbsp (3 oz/85g) butter, cubed
1 large egg, beaten
about 1 tbsp cold water

For the filling

½ cup (4 oz/114g) butter, softened
½ cup (4 oz/100g) superfine sugar
2 large eggs
1 cup plus 1 tbsp (4 oz/100g) almond flour
1 tsp almond extract
4 good tbsp raspberry jam
a few slivered almonds

1 You will need a deep, 8 in loose-bottomed, fluted tart tin.

2 To make the pastry, measure the flour, confectioners' sugar and butter into a food processor. Whizz until breadcrumb stage. Add the egg and water and whizz again until a dough is formed. Roll out thinly on a floured work surface. Line the tin and prick the base and sides. Leave to chill in the fridge for 30 minutes.

3 Preheat the oven to 400°F/Convection 350°F and put a baking sheet in the oven on the shelf just above the center.

4 To make the filling, measure the butter and sugar into a food processor and whizz until light and fluffy. Add the eggs and whizz again. Finally, add the almond flour and extract and whizz one last time.

5 Spread the base of the flan with the jam then pour the filling over the top. Sprinkle with the slivered almonds and place the tin on the hot baking sheet. Bake in the preheated oven for 30–35 minutes, or until the pastry is pale golden brown at the edges and the filling is set.

6 Leave to cool in the tin, then lift out onto a serving plate. Serve cut into wedges.

MAKING TIME 10 MINUTES
CHILLING TIME 30 MINUTES
BAKING TIME 25–30 MINUTES

SUMMER RASPBERRY SHORTBREAD

This looks very good when served for a special coffee morning. Make sure that everyone has a small fork and serve the shortbread with a dollop of thick cream.

SERVES 8

1 cup plus 1 tbsp (4½ oz/125g) all-purpose flour
6 tbsp (3 oz/85g) butter
2½ tbsp (1½ oz/40g) superfine sugar
1½ cups (12 oz/350g) raspberries
3 tbsp redcurrant jelly
heavy cream, whipped, to serve

1 Sift the flour into a bowl. Add the butter and sugar and rub in the butter until the mixture resembles fine breadcrumbs. Knead together, then turn onto a table and knead lightly for 3 minutes until the mixture is smooth.

2 Roll or pat out the shortbread on a baking sheet to a round ¼ in thick and 8 in in diameter. Crimp the edges and leave to chill in the fridge for 30 minutes.

3 Preheat the oven to 325°F/Convection 275°F.

4 Bake in the preheated oven for 25–30 minutes, or until a pale golden brown at the edges.

5 Leave on the baking sheet until quite cold, then lift out onto a serving plate.

6 Arrange the raspberries all over the shortbread.

7 Heat the redcurrant jelly in a small pan until liquified and smooth and then brush it over the fruit and leave to set.

8 Serve the shortbread in wedges with a dollop of thick cream.

MAKING TIME 10 MINUTES
CHILLING TIME 30 MINUTES
BAKING TIME 30–35 MINUTES

TRADITIONAL MOLASSES TART

Molasses tart is one of those favorites that is so easy to prepare and always has the family coming back for second helpings. I try to keep breadcrumbs in the freezer so that they are easily at hand for recipes such as this. There will be a little pastry left over, so use it for a few jam tarts.

SERVES 8

For the shortcrust pastry
1¼ cups (6 oz/175g) all-purpose flour
1 level tbsp confectioners' sugar
6 tbsp (3 oz/85g) butter, cubed
1 large egg, beaten
about 1 tbsp cold water

For the filling
about 9 good tbsp golden syrup (available online)
about ⅔ cup (5 oz/150g) fresh white or brown breadcrumbs
finely grated zest and juice of 1 large lemon

1 You will need an 8 in loose-bottomed, fluted tart tin.

2 To make the pastry, measure the flour, confectioners' sugar and butter into a food processor. Whizz until breadcrumb stage. Add the egg and water and whizz again until a dough is formed. Roll out thinly on a floured work surface. Line the tin and prick the base and sides. Leave to chill in the fridge for 30 minutes.

3 Preheat the oven to 400°F/Convection 350°F.

4 Heat the syrup in a large pan over a medium heat until runny and then stir in the breadcrumbs, lemon zest and juice. (It may be necessary to add a few more breadcrumbs if the mixture looks too runny.)

5 Turn the mixture into the crust, level out the top and bake in the preheated oven for 10 minutes. Reduce the oven temperature to 350°F/Convection 320°F and bake for 20–25 minutes more, or until the tart is cooked.

6 Leave to cool in the tin, then lift out onto a serving plate. Serve cut into wedges.

MAKING TIME 15 MINUTES
CHILLING TIME 6 HOURS

ORANGE CHEESECAKE

A lovely no-bake cheesecake.

SERVES 8

- 1¼ cups (300ml) smooth fresh orange juice from a carton
- 1 x 10 oz (135g) packet orange jelly candies, cubed
- 12 oz (350g) full-fat cream cheese, at room temperature
- 2¼ tbsp (1 oz/25g) superfine sugar
- ½ cup (4 oz/120ml) heavy cream, whipped
- 1 x 10.7 oz (298g) can mandarin segments

For the base

- 5 oz (150g) plain graham crackers crushed
- 2¼ tbsp (1 oz/25g) demerara sugar
- 4 tbsp (2 oz/55g) butter, melted

1 You will need an 8 in loose-bottomed springform cake tin.

2 Measure the orange juice into a saucepan and place over a medium heat until hand hot. Remove from the heat and add the jelly cubes. Stir until dissolved.

3 Pour into a bowl and leave to chill in the fridge until the jelly candies has thickened and is starting to set.

4 Meanwhile, make the base by mixing together the graham crackers, sugar and melted butter. Spread over the base of the cake tin and place in the fridge to set.

5 Measure the cream cheese into a large bowl and whisk with the superfine sugar. Add the almost-set jelly and then fold in the whipped cream. Mix until smooth. Turn into the tin on top of the crumb base and return to the fridge for about 4 hours, until set.

6 When ready to serve, remove the cheesecake from the tin and place it on a serving dish. Drain the mandarins and arrange around the top of the cheesecake.

MAKING TIME 15 MINUTES
BAKING TIME 40 MINUTES

VANILLA BAKED CHEESECAKE

A rich and moist cheesecake.

SERVES 8

- 6 tbsp (3 oz/85g) butter
- 8 to 10 graham crackers, crushed (about 4½ oz/125g)
- 2 (8 oz/226g) packages full-fat cream cheese
- ½ cup (2 oz/50g) all-purpose flour
- 2 tsp vanilla extract
- 2 large eggs
- ½ cup (4 oz/100g) superfine sugar
- ½ cup (4 oz/120ml) heavy cream
- ½ cup (4 oz/150ml) sour cream
- 1 level tbsp confectioners' sugar, sifted
- 1 ripe mango, peeled and finely sliced
- 1 large passion fruit

1 Preheat the oven to 350°F/Convection 320°F. Lightly grease the base of an 8 in loose-bottomed cake or springform tin and line with nonstick baking paper.

2 Melt the butter in a pan over a gentle heat. Remove from the heat and measure in the crackers. Mix together very well.

3 Turn into the tin and press flat over the base using a spoon.

4 Measure the cream cheese and flour into another bowl and beat using an electric hand-held mixer until smooth. Add the vanilla, eggs, sugar and cream and beat again until well blended.

5 Pour over the crumb base and bake in the preheated oven for about 30 minutes, or until well risen and just set around the edges.

6 Remove from the oven and rest for 10 minutes to allow the top of the cheesecake to become level and flat.

7 Return to the oven for a final 10 minutes, or until the cheesecake is just set with a slight wobble in the middle.

8 Loosen the edges, then leave to cool in the tin. When cold, remove from the tin and leave to chill in the fridge.

9 Mix the sour cream and confectioners' sugar together in a small bowl and then spread over the cold cheesecake. Arrange the mango and seeds and pulp of the passion fruit over the top of the cheesecake before serving.

MAKING TIME 10 MINUTES
CHILLING TIME 4 HOURS

THOMAS'S FLAN

This flan is named after my elder son and was one of his favorites to make growing up. Serve it with any fruit that is on hand; blueberries are nice or, if it is summer, use strawberries or raspberries. In winter, canned mandarin oranges look very good.

SERVES 6–8

For the flan case
6 tbsp (3 oz/85g) butter
8 to 10 graham crackers, crushed (about 4½ oz/125g)

For the filling and decoration
1 x 14 oz (397g) can full-fat condensed milk
½ cup (4 oz/120ml) heavy cream
zest and juice of 2 lemons
a selection of fresh fruits, to decorate

1 Line the base and sides of an 8 in loose-bottomed cake or springform tin.

2 Melt the butter in a pan over a gentle heat. Remove from the heat and measure in the crackers. Mix together very well.

3 Turn into the tin and press flat over the base and sides of the tin using a spoon. Leave to chill in the fridge.

4 Meanwhile, to make the topping, measure the condensed milk, cream and lemon juice into a bowl and beat with an electric hand-held mixer until well blended. Pour into the flan crust and level the top.

5 Leave to chill in the fridge for at least 4 hours, until set.

6 When ready to serve, lift out of the tin and decorate with the finely grated lemon zest and fruits of your choice.

MAKING TIME 10 MINUTES
BAKING TIME 45–50 MINUTES

COCONUT AND JAM CAKE

Delicious served warm as dessert.

SERVES 6

4 tbsp (2 oz/55g) butter, softened
¾ cup (6 oz/175g) superfine sugar
4 large eggs
1 cup (4 oz/100g) self-rising flour
2 cups (16 oz/480ml) milk
1¼ cups (2.6 oz/75g) desiccated coconut
4 tbsp raspberry jam
heavy cream, to serve

1 Preheat the oven to 350°F/Convection 320°F and lightly grease a 10 in shallow ovenproof dish.

2 Measure the butter, sugar and eggs into a bowl and beat using an electric hand-held whisk until smooth. Add the flour and whisk again. While whisking, pour the milk in a steady stream to make a smooth batter. Fold in the coconut.

3 Spread a thin layer of jam over the base of the dish and then pour in the batter from a low height.

4 Bake in the preheated oven for 45–50 minutes, or until well risen and golden brown with a slight wobble in the middle.

5 Serve warm with cream.

MAKING TIME 10 MINUTES
BAKING TIME 1 HOUR
COOLING TIME 2 HOURS

RASPBERRY CREAM PAVLOVA

This is really not difficult and does not take too long to make. It needs just an hour, undisturbed, in the oven. You must then turn off the heat and forget it until it is quite cold; do not open the oven door and peep.

SERVES 8

3 large egg whites
¾ cup (6 oz/175g) superfine sugar
1 tsp white vinegar
1 level tsp cornstarch
1 cup (8 oz/225g) fresh raspberries
1¼ cups (10 oz/300ml) heavy cream, whipped
confectioners' sugar, to decorate

1 Preheat the oven to 325°F/Convection 275°F and lay a sheet of silicone paper or nonstick baking paper on a baking sheet and mark an 8 in circle on it.

2 Place the egg whites in a large bowl and beat on high speed with a hand-held mixer until soft peaks form.

3 Add the sugar, a generous spoonful at a time, beating on maximum speed until all the sugar has been added and the meringue is stiff and shiny.

4 Blend the vinegar with the cornstarch in a little bowl until smooth and whisk it into the meringue mixture.

5 Spread the meringue out to cover the circle on the baking sheet—building up the sides so that they are higher than the center. Place in the middle of the preheated oven and immediately turn down the heat to 300°F/Convection 225°F. Bake for about 1 hour, or until the pavlova is a pale creamy color. Turn the oven off and leave in the oven for 1 hour to become cold.

6 Remove from the oven, lift off the paper and place on a serving dish.

7 Keep some of the raspberries back for decoration and put the rest in a large bowl with the cream and lightly fold together.

8 Pile the cream and raspberry mixture into the center of the pavlova and leave to stand for 1 hour in a cool place or fridge before serving. Just before serving, decorate with the reserved raspberries and dredge with a little confectioners' sugar.

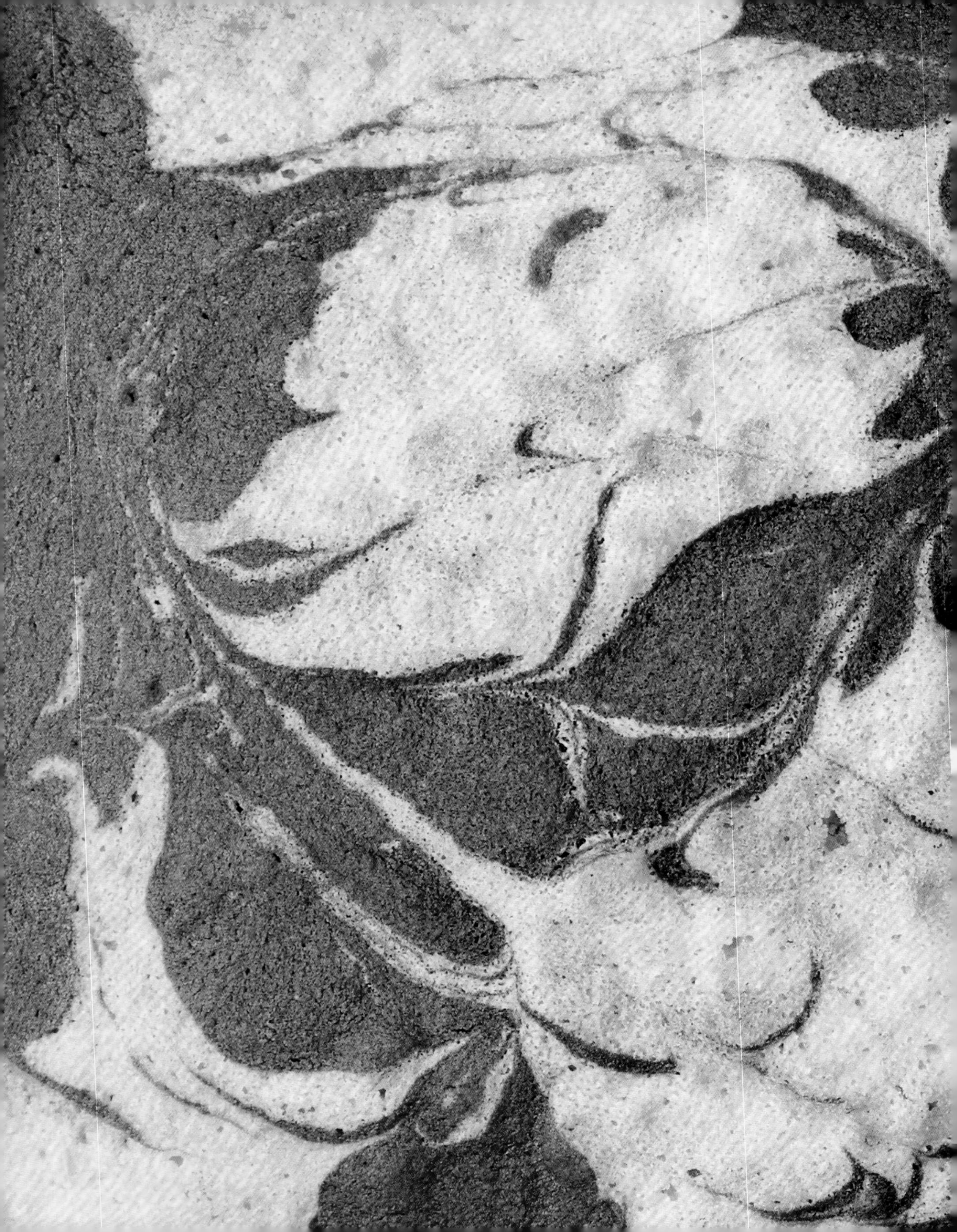

CHAPTER TWO

TRAYBAKES AND FAMILY CAKES

MAKING TIME 10 MINUTES
BAKING TIME 30–35 MINUTES

BASIC TRAYBAKE

The basic recipe is economical and made with large families, coffee mornings and bazaars in mind.

MAKES 16 PIECES

1 cup (8 oz/225g) margarine, from fridge
1 cup (8 oz/225g) superfine sugar
2½ cups (10 oz/275g) self-rising flour
1 level tsp baking powder
4 large eggs
4 tbsp milk

To finish

a little sifted confectioners' sugar (optional)

1 Preheat the oven to 350°F/Convection 320°F. Grease a 12 x 9 in traybake tin and line with nonstick baking paper.

2 Measure all the ingredients into a large bowl and beat with an electric mixer until light and fluffy.

3 Turn the mixture into the tin and level the top. Bake in the preheated oven for 30–35 minutes, or until the cake has shrunk a little from the sides of the tin and springs back when pressed in the center with your fingertips.

4 Leave to cool in the tin.

5 Sprinkle with confectioners' sugar, if desired, and cut into 16 pieces.

VARIATION: VANILLA TRAYBAKE

Add 1 teaspoon of vanilla extract to the traybake ingredients and continue to prepare as above.

MAKING TIME 10 MINUTES
BAKING TIME 30–35 MINUTES

FRUIT TRAYBAKE

Adding some dried fruit to the basic traybake recipe gives a lovely and easy alternative. Use whatever you have in the cupboard, though currants work particularly well.

MAKES 16 PIECES

1 cup (8 oz/225g) margarine, from fridge
1 cup (8 oz/225g) superfine sugar
2½ cups (10 oz/275g) self-rising flour
1 level tsp baking powder
4 large eggs
4 tbsp milk
¾ cup (7 oz/200g) sultanas
½ cup (4 oz/100g) ready-to-eat dried apricots, finely chopped
1 level tbsp demerara sugar

1 Preheat the oven to 350°F/Convection 320°F. Grease a 12 x 9 in traybake tin and line with nonstick baking paper.

2 Measure all the ingredients except the dried fruit and demerara sugar into a large bowl and beat with an electric mixer until well blended. Stir in the sultanas and apricots.

3 Turn the mixture into the tin and level the top. Bake in the preheated oven for 30–35 minutes, or until the cake has shrunk a little from the sides of the tin and springs back when pressed in the center with your fingertips. Halfway through the baking time, remove the cake from the oven and sprinkle the top with the demerara sugar.

4 Cool completely in the tin.

5 Cut into 16 pieces to serve.

MAKING TIME 10 MINUTES
BAKING TIME 30–35 MINUTES

VANILLA AND CHOCOLATE MARBLE TRAYBAKE

This is a lovely variation on the basic traybake—a visual treat perfect for the school bake sale.

MAKES 16 PIECES

- 1 cup (8 oz/225g) margarine, from fridge
- 1 cup (8 oz/225g) superfine sugar
- 2½ cups (10 oz/275g) self-rising flour
- 1 level tsp baking powder
- 4 large eggs
- 4 tbsp milk
- 1 tsp vanilla extract
- 1 tbsp (1 oz/25g) cocoa powder

To finish

- a little sifted confectioners' sugar (optional)

1 Preheat the oven to 350°F/Convection 320°F. Grease a 12 x 9 in traybake tin and line with nonstick baking paper.

2 Measure all the ingredients except the cocoa into a large bowl and beat well with an electric mixer until light and fluffy. Place half the mixture in another bowl and add the cocoa powder. Mix until well blended.

3 Place large spoonfuls of both cake mixtures in the tin, then swirl the two colors together using a skewer to create a marbled effect.

4 Bake in the preheated oven for 30–35 minutes, or until the cake has shrunk a little from the sides of the tin and springs back when pressed in the center with your fingertips.

5 Cool completely in the tin.

6 Sprinkle with confectioners' sugar, if desired, and cut into 16 pieces.

MAKING TIME 10 MINUTES
BAKING TIME 35–40 MINUTES

LEMON DRIZZLE TRAYBAKE

It's important to spoon the glaze on the cake while it's still warm so the lemon juice soaks in properly.

MAKES 16 PIECES

- 1 cup (8 oz/225g) margarine, from fridge
- 1 cup (8 oz/225g) superfine sugar
- 2½ cups (10 oz/275g) self-rising flour
- 1 level tsp baking powder
- 4 large eggs
- 4 tbsp milk
- finely grated zest of 2 lemons

For the glaze

- juice of 2 lemons
- ¾ cup (6 oz/175g) granulated sugar

1 Preheat the oven to 350°F/Convection 320°F. Grease a 12 x 9 in traybake tin and line with nonstick baking paper.

2 Measure all the ingredients into a large bowl and beat with an electric mixer until well blended.

3 Turn the mixture into the tin and level the top. Bake in the preheated oven for 35–40 minutes, or until the cake has shrunk a little from the sides of the tin and springs back when pressed in the center with your fingertips.

4 While the cake is baking, make the glaze. Mix the lemon juice and sugar together in a bowl and stir to a runny consistency.

5 As soon as the traybake comes out of the oven, pour the lemon and sugar glaze over the surface of the warm cake, spreading to cover and leave to set.

6 When completely cool, cut into 16 pieces.

MAKING TIME 10 MINUTES
BAKING TIME 35–40 MINUTES

SPICED MOLASSES TRAYBAKE

When the cake is baked and cooled, it looks nice if sprinkled with sifted confectioners' sugar.

MAKES 16 PIECES

- 1 cup (8 oz/225g) margarine, from fridge
- ½ cup plus 1 tbsp (4½ oz/115g) superfine sugar
- 2½ cups (10 oz/275g) self-rising flour
- 1 level tsp baking powder
- 4 large eggs
- 4 tbsp milk
- ¾ cup (7 oz/200g) black molasses
- 1½ level tsp pumpkin pie spice

To finish

- a little sifted confectioners' sugar (optional)

1 Preheat the oven to 350°F/Convection 320°F. Grease a 12 x 9 in traybake tin and line with nonstick baking paper.

2 Measure all the ingredients into a large bowl and beat with an electric mixer until well blended.

3 Turn the mixture into the tin and level the top. Bake in the preheated oven for 35–40 minutes, or until the cake has shrunk a little from the sides of the tin and springs back when pressed in the center with your fingertips.

4 Cool completely in the tin.

5 Sprinkle with confectioners' sugar, if desired, and cut into 16 pieces.

MAKING TIME 10 MINUTES
BAKING TIME 30 MINUTES

ICED CHERRY TRAYBAKE

Celebrate summer by using fresh cherries in season.

MAKES 16 PIECES

1 cup (8 oz/225g) margarine, from fridge
1 cup (8 oz/225g) superfine sugar
2½ cups (10 oz/275g) self-rising flour
1 level tsp baking powder
4 large eggs
4 tbsp milk

For the icing

6 tbsp (3 oz/85g) butter, softened
2 cups (8 oz/225g) confectioners' sugar, sifted
1–2 tbsp milk
1 tsp vanilla extract

To finish

16 natural glacé cherries, halved

1 Preheat the oven to 350°F/Convection 320°F. Grease a 12 x 9 in traybake tin and line with nonstick baking paper.

2 Measure all the cake ingredients into a large bowl and beat with an electric mixer until well blended.

3 Turn the mixture into the tin and level the top. Bake in the preheated oven for about 30 minutes, or until the cake has shrunk a little from the sides of the tin and springs back when pressed in the center with your fingertips.

4 Cool completely in the tin.

5 Measure the icing ingredients into a bowl and beat with an electric mixer until well blended. Spread over the top of the cake, mark into 16 segments and decorate each piece with 2 glacé cherry halves.

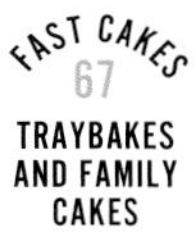

MAKING TIME 15 MINUTES
BAKING TIME 30–35 MINUTES

LEMON AND LIME TRAYBAKE

This is a lovely and citrusy traybake.

MAKES 16 PIECES

1 cup (8 oz/225g) margarine, from fridge
1 cup (8 oz/225g) superfine sugar
2½ cups (10 oz/275g) self-rising flour
4 large eggs
1 level tsp baking powder
2 level tbsp lemon curd
finely grated zest of 1 large lemon
finely grated zest of 1 large lime

For the icing

2½ cups (10½ oz/300g) confectioners' sugar, sifted
3–4 tbsp lemon and lime juice

1 Preheat the oven to 350°F/Convection 320°F. Grease a 12 x 9 in traybake tin and line with nonstick baking paper.

2 Measure the margarine, superfine sugar, flour, eggs, baking powder, lemon curd and half of the lemon and lime zests into a mixing bowl. Beat together using an electric mixer until light and fluffy.

3 Turn the mixture into the tin and level the top. Bake in the preheated oven for 30–35 minutes, or until well risen and the top of the sponge springs back when lightly pressed with a finger.

4 Cool completely in the tin.

5 To make the icing, measure the confectioners' sugar and lemon and lime juices into a bowl. Whisk until smooth, then spread over the cake.

6 Sprinkle with the remaining lemon and lime zest before cutting into 16 pieces.

MAKING TIME 10 MINUTES
BAKING TIME 30–35 MINUTES

POPPY SEED AND LEMON TRAYBAKE

Full of zesty lemon flavor.

MAKES 16 PIECES

1 cup (8 oz/225g) margarine, from fridge
1 cup (8 oz/225g) superfine sugar
2½ cups (10 oz/275g) self-rising flour
1 level tsp baking powder
4 large eggs
4 tbsp milk
finely grated zest of 2 lemons
2 level tbsp poppy seeds

For the glaze
juice of 2 lemons
¾ cup (7 oz/200g) granulated sugar

1 Preheat the oven to 350°F/Convection 320°F. Grease a 12 x 9 in traybake tin and line with nonstick baking paper.

2 Measure all the ingredients except the poppy seeds into a large bowl and beat with an electric mixer until light and fluffy. Fold in the poppy seeds, turn the mixture into the tin and level the top.

3 Bake in the preheated oven for 30–35 minutes, or until the cake has shrunk a little from the sides of the tin and springs back when pressed in the center with your fingertips.

4 While the cake is baking, make the glaze. Mix the lemon juice and sugar together in a bowl and stir to a runny consistency.

5 As soon as the traybake comes out of the oven, pour the lemon glaze over the surface of the warm cake, spreading to cover, and leave to set.

6 When completely cool, cut into 16 pieces.

MAKING TIME 10 MINUTES
BAKING TIME 40–45 MINUTES

COCONUT AND FRUIT TRAYBAKE

Ideal to include in a lunch box or to take on a picnic.

MAKES 16 PIECES

- 1 cup (8 oz/225g) margarine, from fridge
- 2 cups (8 oz/225g) self-rising flour
- 2 level tsp pumpkin pie spice
- 2½ cups (5.3 oz/150g) desiccated coconut
- 1 cup (8 oz/225g) light muscovado sugar
- 4 large eggs
- 2 tbsp milk
- ¾ cup (7 oz/200g) sultanas
- ½ cup (4 oz/100g) seedless raisins
- confectioners' sugar, to dust

1 Preheat the oven to 350°F/Convection 320°F. Grease a 12 x 9 in traybake tin and line with nonstick baking paper.

2 Place all the ingredients except the dried fruit and confectioners' sugar in a bowl and beat with an electric mixer until light and fluffy. Stir in the sultanas and raisins.

3 Turn the mixture into the tin and level the top. Bake in the preheated oven for 40–45 minutes, or until golden brown and springing back when lightly pressed with your fingertips.

4 Cool completely in the tin.

5 Dust with confectioners' sugar and cut into 16 pieces.

MAKING TIME 10 MINUTES
BAKING TIME 40 MINUTES

COFFEE FUDGE TRAYBAKE

This traybake has a very mild coffee flavor that, strangely enough, is popular with children.

MAKES 20 PIECES
12 tbsp (6 oz/170g) margarine, from fridge
¾ cup (6 oz/175g) superfine sugar
3 large eggs
1 tbsp coffee extract
1¼ cups (6 oz/175g) self-rising flour
¾ level tsp baking powder

For the icing
6 tbsp (3 oz/85g) butter, softened
2 cups (8 oz/225g) confectioners' sugar, sifted
1 tbsp milk
1 tbsp coffee extract

1 Preheat the oven to 320°F/Convection 270°F. Grease a 12 x 9 in traybake tin and line with nonstick baking paper.

2 Measure the traybake ingredients into a bowl and beat well with an electric mixer until well blended.

3 Turn the mixture into the tin and level the top. Bake in the preheated oven for 40 minutes, or until the cake is well risen and shrinking away from the sides of the tin. The cake will spring back when lightly pressed with your fingertips.

4 Cool completely in the tin.

5 To make the icing, put the butter, confectioners' sugar, milk and coffee extract in a bowl and beat until smooth. Spread over the cake and cut into 20 pieces.

MAKING TIME 10 MINUTES
BAKING TIME 30–35 MINUTES

CONFETTI TRAYBAKE

This looks so pretty—it's a simple, fast cake for school fêtes or coffee mornings.

MAKES 20 PIECES

1 cup (8 oz/225g) margarine, from fridge
1 cup (8 oz/225g) superfine sugar
2½ cups (10 oz/275g) self-rising flour
1 level tsp baking powder
4 large eggs
4 tbsp milk
1 tsp vanilla extract

To finish

2½ cups (10½ oz/300g) confectioners' sugar
3 tbsp boiling water
2 level tbsp colored sprinkles

1 Preheat the oven to 350°F/Convection 320°F. Grease a 12 x 9 in traybake tin and line with nonstick baking paper.

2 Measure all the traybake ingredients into a large bowl and beat with an electric mixer until light and fluffy.

3 Turn the mixture into the tin and level the top. Bake in the preheated oven for 30–35 minutes, or until the cake has shrunk a little from the sides of the tin and springs back when pressed in the center with your fingertips.

4 Cool completely in the tin.

5 Mix the confectioners' sugar and water together in a bowl to make a smooth paste. Spread over the cold cake and top with the sprinkles. Cut into 20 pieces.

MAKING TIME 10 MINUTES
BAKING TIME 30–35 MINUTES

BLUEBERRY AND VANILLA TRAYBAKE

A modern classic combination of flavors.

MAKES 16 PIECES

- 1 cup (8 oz/225g) margarine, from fridge
- 1 cup (8 oz/225g) superfine sugar
- 2½ cups (10 oz/275g) self-rising flour
- 1 level tsp baking powder
- 4 large eggs
- 4 tbsp milk
- 1 tsp vanilla extract

For the icing

- 4 tbsp (2 oz/55g) butter, softened
- 1 cup (4 oz/100g) confectioners' sugar
- 1 tsp vanilla extract
- 9 oz (250g) full-fat mascarpone cheese

To finish

- 1 cup (8 oz/225g) fresh blueberries

1 Preheat the oven to 350°F/Convection 320°F. Grease a 12 x 9 in traybake tin and line with nonstick baking paper.

2 Measure all the traybake ingredients into a large bowl and beat with an electric mixer until light and fluffy.

3 Turn the mixture into the tin and level the top. Bake in the preheated oven for 30–35 minutes, or until the cake has shrunk a little from the sides of the tin and springs back when pressed in the center with your fingertips.

4 Cool completely in the tin.

5 To make the icing, whisk the butter and confectioners' sugar together in a bowl. Add the vanilla and mascarpone and whisk again until smooth. Spread over the top of the traybake, decorate with the blueberries and cut into 16 pieces.

MAKING TIME 10 MINUTES
BAKING TIME 30–35 MINUTES

COFFEE AND WALNUT TRAYBAKE

A traybake version of the family favorite.

MAKES 16 PIECES

2 level tbsp instant coffee granules
2 tbsp boiling water
1 cup (8 oz/225g) margarine, from fridge
1 cup (8 oz/225g) superfine, sugar
2½ cups (10 oz/275g) self-rising flour
1 level tsp baking powder
4 large eggs
4 tbsp milk

To finish

1 level tbsp instant coffee granules
1 tbsp boiling water
½ cup (4 oz/114g) butter, softened
1¼ cups (6 oz/175g) confectioners' sugar
1 tbsp milk
¼ cup (2 oz/50g) walnuts, chopped

1 Preheat the oven to 350°F/Convection 320°F. Grease a 12 x 9 in traybake tin and line with nonstick baking paper.

2 Measure the instant coffee and boiling water into a large mixing bowl. Stir until dissolved. Leave to cool for 2–3 minutes.

3 Add the remaining cake ingredients to the bowl and beat with an electric mixer until light and fluffy.

4 Turn the mixture into the tin and level the top. Bake in the preheated oven for 30–35 minutes, or until the cake has shrunk a little from the sides of the tin and springs back when pressed in the center with your fingertips.

5 Cool completely in the tin.

6 To make the icing, measure the instant coffee and boiling water into a mixing bowl. Stir until dissolved. Leave to cool for 2–3 minutes. Add all of the remaining ingredients except the walnuts to the bowl and beat using an electric mixer until pale and creamy, then spread over the cake.

7 Sprinkle with the walnuts and cut into 16 pieces to serve.

MAKING TIME 15 MINUTES
BAKING TIME 1 HOUR

GINGER TRAYBAKE WITH COFFEE ICING

Lovely and moist, this cake keeps well in an airtight container. The brown sugar and molasses give the cake a slightly denser sponge, rather than it being light.

MAKES 18 PIECES

½ cup (4 oz/114g) margarine, from fridge
⅓ cup (3 oz/75g) black molasses
⅓ cup (3 oz/75g) golden syrup (available online)
⅓ cup (3 oz/75g) light muscovado sugar
3 level tsp ground ginger
2½ cups (10½ oz/300g) self-rising flour
⅓ cup (3½ oz/100ml) milk
3 large eggs

For the icing

2 cups (8 oz/225g) cofectioners' sugar, sifted
2 tsp coffee extract
about 2½ tbsp water

1 Preheat the oven to 320°F/Convection 270°F. Grease a 12 x 9 in traybake tin and line with nonstick baking paper.

2 Measure the margarine, molasses, golden syrup and sugar into a pan and heat gently until the margarine has melted.

3 Measure the ginger and flour into a bowl and pour over the melted mixture. Add the milk and eggs and beat with an electric mixer until thoroughly blended. Pour into the tin.

4 Bake in the preheated oven for about 1 hour, or until well risen and the top springs back when lightly pressed with your fingertips.

5 Leave to cool in the tin for a few moments then turn out, remove the paper and finish cooling on a wire rack.

6 To make the icing, measure the confectioners' sugar into a bowl, add the coffee extract and sufficient water to give a smooth icing. Spread evenly over the top of the cake and leave to set.

7 Cut into 18 pieces to serve.

MAKING TIME 15 MINUTES
BAKING TIME 30–35 MINUTES

SPICED TOFFEE TRAYBAKE

A lovely traybake for a coffee morning or bake sale.

MAKES 16 PIECES

1 cup (8 oz/225g) margarine, from fridge
1 cup (8 oz/225g) light muscovado sugar
2½ cups (10 oz/275g) self-rising flour
1 level tsp baking powder
4 large eggs
2 tbsp milk
2 tbsp molasses
1 level tsp ground ginger
½ level tsp pumpkin pie spice
1 level tsp ground cinnamon

For the icing

½ cup (4 oz/114g) butter, softened
1¼ cups (6 oz/175g) confectioners' sugar
1 tbsp (1 oz/25g) light muscovado sugar
1 tsp vanilla extract
1 tbsp milk
1 level tsp ground cinnamon

1 Preheat the oven to 350°F/Convection 320°F. Grease a 12 x 9 in traybake tin and line with nonstick baking paper.

2 Measure all the traybake ingredients into a large bowl and beat with an electric mixer until light and fluffy.

3 Turn the mixture into the tin and level the top. Bake in the preheated oven for 30–35 minutes, or until the cake has shrunk a little from the sides of the tin and springs back when pressed in the center with your fingertips.

4 Cool completely in the tin.

5 To make the icing, measure all of the ingredients into a large bowl and beat with an electric mixer until pale and creamy. Spread over the cold cake and cut into 16 pieces to serve.

MAKING TIME 10 MINUTES
BAKING TIME 35–40 MINUTES

RED VELVET BROWNIE TRAYBAKE

This has a heavier texture to the other traybakes in this chapter, which makes it more like a brownie. It is delicious and was one of the favorite bakes when we were photographing the recipes for the book!

MAKES 18 PIECES

- 10½ oz (300g) bittersweet or semisweet chocolate, broken into pieces
- ½ cup plus 6 tbsp (7 oz/200g) butter
- ¾ cup (7 oz/200g) superfine sugar
- 4 large eggs
- 1 tsp vanilla extract
- 1¼ cups (5 oz/150g) self-rising flour
- 1 tbsp (½ oz/15g) red gel coloring

For the icing

- 4 tbsp (2 oz/55g) butter, softened
- ¼ cup (2 oz/50g) full-fat cream cheese
- 1¼ cups (5 oz/150g) confectioners' sugar
- ½ tsp vanilla extract

1 Preheat the oven to 350°F/Convection 320°F. Grease a 12 x 9 in traybake tin and line with nonstick baking paper.

2 Measure the chocolate and butter into a heatproof bowl. Melt over a pan of simmering water until smooth and runny.

3 Remove the bowl from the heat and add the sugar, eggs, vanilla and flour. Beat with an electric mixer until well blended and smooth. Stir in the red gel.

4 Turn the mixture into the tin and level the top. Bake in the preheated oven for 35–40 minutes, or until risen and a crust has formed on the surface. The middle should feel just firm when pressed with your fingertips.

5 Cool completely in the tin. The brownie may dip slightly in the center.

6 To make the icing, measure all the ingredients into a large bowl and beat using an electric mixer until pale and creamy. Spread over the brownie and swirl the top.

7 Cut into 18 pieces to serve.

MAKING TIME 10 MINUTES
BAKING TIME 35 MINUTES

ROYAL GINGER SQUARES

If you have had a jar of candied ginger on the shelf for a while, this is a good way of putting it to use. The squares are topped with a simple ginger icing.

MAKES 20 SQUARES

12 tbsp (6 oz/170g) margarine, from fridge
⅔ cup (6 oz/175g) light muscovado sugar
1½ cups (6 oz/175g) self-rising flour
¾ level tsp baking powder
1½ level tsp ground ginger
3 large eggs
1½ oz (40g) candied ginger, very finely chopped

For the topping

1½ cups (6 oz/175g) confectioners' sugar, sifted
3–4 tbsp ginger syrup from the jar

1 Preheat the oven to 350°F/Convection 320°F. Grease a 12 x 9 in traybake tin and line with nonstick baking paper.

2 Measure the margarine, sugar, flour, baking powder, ginger and eggs into a large bowl and beat with an electric mixer until well blended.

3 Turn the mixture into the tin, level the top and bake in the preheated oven for about 20 minutes. Sprinkle over the finely chopped ginger and continue cooking for 15 minutes more, or until the sponge is golden brown and springs back when pressed in the center with your fingertips.

4 Cool completely in the tin, then turn out, remove the paper and finish cooling on a wire rack.

5 To make the icing, blend the confectioners' sugar with the ginger syrup until smooth—loosen with a few drops of water, if necessary. Drizzle or spoon over the cake and leave to set.

6 Cut into 20 squares to serve.

MAKING TIME 10 MINUTES
BAKING TIME 30 MINUTES

BUTTERSCOTCH CAKE

A simple sponge with a very tasty icing on top. It is ideal for cutting into squares or pieces to serve at a coffee morning.

MAKES 24 PIECES

1 cup (8 oz/225g) margarine, from fridge
1 cup (8 oz/225g) light muscovado sugar
4 large eggs
2 cups (8 oz/225g) self-rising flour
1 level tsp baking powder

For the icing

½ cup (4 oz/114g) butter, softened
1½ cups (6 oz/175g) confectioners' sugar
1 tsp vanilla extract
1 tbsp (1 oz/25g) light muscovado sugar
2 tbsp milk

1 Preheat the oven to 350°F/Convection 320°F. Grease a 12 x 9 in traybake tin and line with nonstick baking paper.

2 Measure all the traybake ingredients into a bowl and beat with an electric mixer until light and fluffy.

3 Turn the mixture into the tin, level the top and bake in the preheated oven for about 30 minutes, or until well risen and golden brown. The cake will have shrunk slightly from the sides of the tin.

4 Cool completely in the tin.

5 To make the icing, measure all of the ingredients into a bowl and whisk together until light and creamy. Spread over the surface of the cake.

6 Cut into 24 pieces to serve.

MAKING TIME 10 MINUTES
BAKING TIME 35–40 MINUTES

CRUNCHY HAZELNUT PIECES

The crunchy topping sinks slightly into the cake during baking and gives a lovely flavor to a simple sponge mixture.

MAKES 18 PIECES

- 12 tbsp (6 oz/170g) margarine, from fridge
- ⅔ cup (6 oz/175g) superfine sugar
- 3 large eggs
- 2 cups (8 oz/225g) self-rising flour

For the topping

- 4 tbsp (2 oz/55g) butter
- ⅔ cup (6 oz/175g) demerara sugar
- 2 level tsp ground cinnamon
- 3 level tbsp all-purpose flour
- ¼ cup (2 oz/50g) roasted hazelnuts, chopped

1 Preheat the oven to 350°F/Convection 320°F. Grease a 12 x 9 in traybake tin and line with nonstick baking paper.

2 To make the topping, melt the butter in a small saucepan then remove the pan from the heat and add all the remaining ingredients. Leave to cool.

3 Measure all the traybake ingredients into a bowl and beat with an electric mixer until light and fluffy.

4 Turn the mixture into the tin, level the top and sprinkle with the topping. Bake in the preheated oven for 35–40 minutes, or until the mixture is well risen and has shrunk from the sides of the tin.

5 Cool completely in the tin.

6 Cut into 18 pieces to serve.

MAKING TIME 5 MINUTES
BAKING TIME 30–35 MINUTES

HONEY CAKE

A simple tasty cake that is made all in one saucepan—nice and easy on the washing up!

MAKES 16 PIECES

⅔ cup (5 oz/140g) margarine, from fridge
½ cup (4 oz/100g) dark or light muscovado sugar
½ cup (150ml) clear honey
1 tbsp milk
2 large eggs
1¾ cups (7 oz/200g) self-rising flour
a few slivered almonds

1 Preheat the oven to 350°F/Convection 320°F. Grease a 12 x 9 in traybake tin and line with nonstick baking paper.

2 Put the margarine, sugar, honey and milk in a saucepan and heat gently until the spread has melted and the sugar has dissolved. Set aside to cool.

3 Beat the eggs into the cooled honey mixture one at a time then stir in the flour.

4 Pour the mixture into the tin and sprinkle the top with almonds. Bake in the preheated oven for 30–35 minutes, or until well risen and the cake has shrunk back from the sides of the tin.

5 Turn out, remove the paper, then leave to cool on a wire rack.

6 Cut into 16 pieces and store in an airtight container.

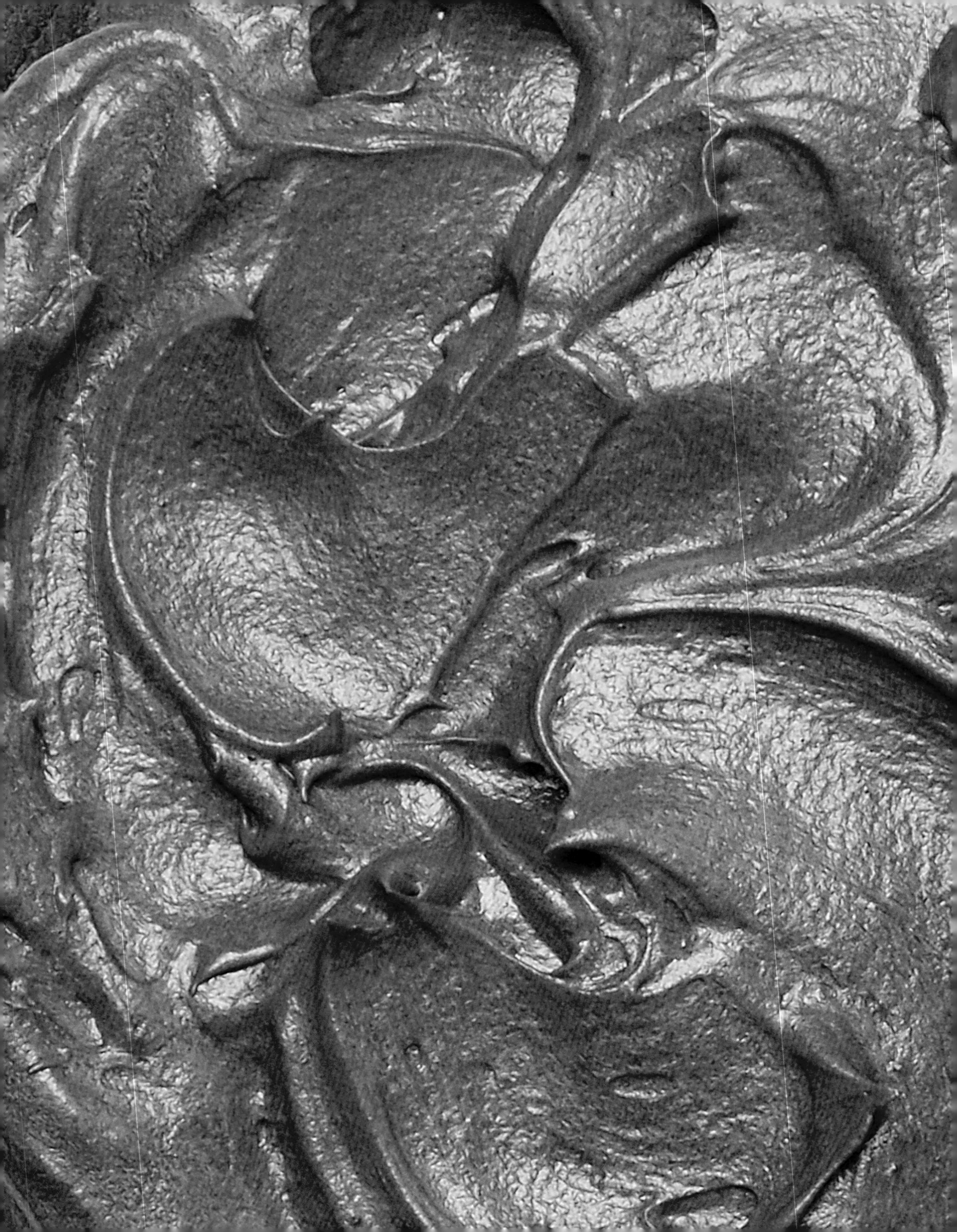

CHAPTER THREE

CHOCOLATE BAKES

MAKING TIME 5 MINUTES
BAKING TIME 25–30 MINUTES

CLASSIC CHOCOLATE SPONGE SANDWICH

A classic chocolate sponge—such an easy and quick cake.

SERVES 8

- 2 good tbsp cocoa powder
- 4 tbsp hot water
- 1 cup (8 oz/225g) margarine, from fridge
- 1 cup (8 oz/225g) superfine sugar, plus extra to sprinkle
- 4 large eggs
- 2 cups (8 oz/225g) self-rising flour
- 1 level tsp baking powder
- bittersweet or semisweet chocolate, grated or curled, to decorate

For the icing

- 6 tbsp (3 oz/85g) butter, softened
- 2 cups (8 oz/225g) confectioners' sugar, sifted

1 Preheat the oven to 350°F/Convection 320°F. Grease two 8 in round sandwich tins and line the bases with nonstick baking paper.

2 Blend the cocoa with the water in a small bowl and leave to cool.

3 Measure the margarine, sugar, eggs, flour and baking powder into a large mixing bowl, add the cooled cocoa liquid and beat with an electric mixer until thoroughly blended.

4 Divide the mixture between the tins, level out evenly and bake in the preheated oven for 25–30 minutes, or until well risen and the tops of the sponges spring back when lightly pressed with your fingertips.

5 Leave to cool in the tins for a few minutes, then turn out, remove the paper and finish cooling on a wire rack.

6 To make the icing, blend the butter with the confectioners' sugar and use half to sandwich the cakes together when they are completely cooled. Use the other half to ice the top.

7 Lift onto a serving plate and decorate with curls or gratings of chocolate.

MAKING TIME 10 MINUTES
BAKING TIME 30–35 MINUTES

CAN'T-GO-WRONG CHOCOLATE CAKE

A moist chocolate cake that really can't go wrong and keeps well.

SERVES 8

- 1¼ cups (6½ oz/190g) all-purpose flour
- 2 level tbsp cocoa powder
- 1 level tsp baking soda
- 1 level tsp baking powder
- ⅔ cup (5 oz/150g) superfine sugar
- 2 tbsp golden syrup (available online)
- 2 large eggs
- ½ cup (150ml) sunflower oil
- ½ cup (4 oz/120ml) milk

For the icing

- 4 tbsp (2 oz/55g) butter
- 4 level tbsp cocoa powder, sifted
- 3 tbsp milk
- 1¼ cups (5 oz/150g) confectioners' sugar, sifted

1 Preheat the oven to 320°F/Convection 270°F. Grease two 8 in round sandwich tins and line the bases with nonstick baking paper.

2 Sift the dry ingredients into a large bowl and then make a well in the center. Add the syrup, eggs, oil and milk. Beat well with an electric mixer until thoroughly blended.

3 Pour the mixture into the tins and bake in the preheated oven for 30–35 minutes, or until the cake springs back when lightly pressed with your fingertips.

4 Turn out onto a wire rack, remove the paper and leave to cool.

5 To make the icing, melt the butter in a small pan over a gentle heat. Add the cocoa, stir to blend and cook gently for 1 minute. Stir in the milk and confectioners' sugar, remove from the heat and mix very well. Set aside, stirring occasionally, until the icing thickens.

6 Sandwich the cakes with half the icing and then use the remainder to ice the top, swirling with a knife to give an attractive appearance.

MAKING TIME 5 MINUTES
BAKING TIME 20–25 MINUTES

SIMPLE CHOCOLATE CAKE WITH FUDGE ICING

A fabulous chocolate cake. This delicious cake can be made in an 8 in aluminum pan, allowed to cool in the pan and then iced. This makes it perfect to take on a picnic or to sell at a bake sale.

SERVES 8

- 2 level tbsp cocoa powder
- 2 tbsp hot water
- ½ cup (4 oz/114g) margarine, from fridge
- ½ cup (4 oz/100g) superfine sugar
- 2 large eggs
- 1 cup (4 oz/100g) self-rising flour
- 1 level tsp baking powder

For the icing

- 3½ tbsp (1 oz/25g) cocoa powder, sifted
- 3 tbsp (1½ oz/40g) butter, softened
- 2–3 tbsp milk
- 1 cup (4 oz/100g) confectioners' sugar, sifted

1 Preheat the oven to 350°F/Convection 320°F. Grease a deep, 8 in cake tin and line with nonstick baking paper. If using an aluminum container, grease this well.

2 Blend the cocoa with the hot water in a large bowl and leave to cool. Add the remaining cake ingredients to the bowl and beat with an electric mixer until light and fluffy.

3 Spoon into the tin and bake in the preheated oven for 20–25 minutes, or until the cake has shrunk slightly from the sides of the tin and springs back when lightly pressed with a finger.

4 Turn out, remove the paper and cool completely on a wire rack.

5 To make the icing, measure the cocoa, butter, milk and confectioners' sugar into a bowl. Beat well to a light, smooth consistency.

6 Spread over the top of the cake and swirl attractively with a round-bladed knife. Leave to set before serving.

MAKING TIME 20 MINUTES
BAKING TIME 25 MINUTES

MELT-IN-THE-MOUTH CHOCOLATE DESSERT CAKE

This is a heavenly, light chocolate cake to serve with a fork. The cake itself contains no flour and has a good chocolate flavor. Do expect it to sink slightly after cooling.

SERVES 8

- 6 large eggs
- ⅔ cup (5 oz/150g) superfine sugar
- ½ cup (2 oz/50g) cocoa powder, sifted

For the filling and topping

- 1¼ cup (10 oz/300ml) heavy cream, whipped
- ¼ cup (1 oz/25g) confectioners' sugar, sifted (optional)
- wafer-thin mint chocolates, to decorate (optional)

1 Preheat the oven to 350°F/Convection 320°F. Grease two 8 in round sandwich tins and line the bases with nonstick baking paper.

2 Separate the eggs by putting the whites in a large bowl and the yolks in a smaller bowl. Add the superfine sugar to the yolks and beat with an electric mixer until thick.

3 Whisk the egg whites with an electric whisk until stiff peaks form. Add 2 tablespoons of the whisked whites to the yolk mixture, mix thoroughly, then add this to the whites and gently fold in until thoroughly blended. Finally, fold in the cocoa powder.

4 Divide the mixture between the tins, level out evenly and bake in the preheated oven for about 25 minutes, or until just beginning to shrink back from the sides of the tins. They will rise but will drop back down toward the end of the baking.

5 Leave to cool in the tins for about 5 minutes then turn out, remove the paper and finish cooling on a wire rack.

6 Sweeten the cream with the confectioners' sugar, if using, then sandwich the cakes together with half the cream and spread the remainder on top.

7 Break the mint thins in half, if using, and arrange around the top of the cake before serving.

MAKING TIME 10 MINUTES
BAKING TIME 40 MINUTES

AMERICAN CHOCOLATE CAKE

A really large, moist chocolate cake that is quick to make.

SERVES 8

- 2½ cups (10 oz/275g) self-rising flour
- 3 level tbsp cocoa powder
- ⅔ cup (6 oz/175g) superfine sugar
- 1 level tsp baking soda
- 1¼ cup (10 oz/300ml) milk
- ¾ cup (150ml) sunflower oil
- 3 tbsp golden syrup (available online)
- ½ tsp vanilla extract

For the icing

- 3½ tbsp (1 oz/25g) cocoa powder, sifted
- 2 tbsp (1 oz/30g) butter, softened
- 1¾ cups (7 oz/200g) confectioners' sugar, sifted
- 2–3 tbsp milk

1 Preheat the oven to 350°F/Convection 320°F. Grease two 8 in round sandwich tins and line the bases with nonstick baking paper.

2 Sift the flour, cocoa and superfine sugar into a bowl and make a well in the center.

3 Dissolve the baking soda in 1 tablespoon of the milk and then pour this into the flour with the remaining milk, oil, syrup and vanilla extract and beat with an electric mixer to make a smooth batter.

4 Pour the mixture into the tins and bake in the preheated oven for about 40 minutes, or until the cakes spring back when lightly pressed with a fingertip.

5 Turn out onto a wire rack and leave to cool.

6 To make the icing, place the cocoa, butter and confectioners' sugar in a bowl and beat together until smooth, adding the milk to loosen. Use to sandwich the cakes together.

MAKING TIME 10 MINUTES
BAKING TIME 25–30 MINUTES

MILK CHOCOLATE CAKE

A richer chocolate cake. Use a small can of evaporated milk; this will give you enough for both the cake and the icing.

SERVES 8

1¾ cups (7 oz/200g) self-rising flour
1 cup (8 oz/225g) superfine sugar
3½ tbsp (1 oz/25g) cocoa powder, sifted
½ cup (4 oz/100g) margarine, from fridge
2 large eggs
⅔ cup (5 oz/150ml) evaporated milk

For the icing

1 tbsp (1 oz/30g) margarine
3½ tbsp (1 oz/25g) cocoa powder, sifted
2 tbsp evaporated milk
1 cup (4 oz/125g) confectioners' sugar, sifted
bittersweet or semisweet chocolate, grated into shards, to decorate (optional)

For the filling

½ cup (4 oz/120ml) heavy cream, lightly whipped

1 Preheat the oven to 350°F/Convection 320°F. Grease two 8 in round sandwich tins and line the bases with nonstick baking paper.

2 Place all the cake ingredients together in a bowl and beat with an electric mixer until light and fluffy.

3 Divide the mixture between the two tins, level out evenly and bake in the preheated oven for 25–30 minutes, or until the cakes are well risen and have shrunk slightly from the sides of the tin. They should spring back when lightly pressed with a fingertip.

4 Turn out and cool completely on a wire rack.

5 To make the icing, put the margarine and cocoa in a saucepan and heat gently until the margarine has melted, stirring continuously. Remove from the heat and beat in the evaporated milk and confectioners' sugar until the mixture is thick.

6 Sandwich the cakes together with the whipped cream, then spread the icing over the top of the cake. Sprinkle with chocolate shards, if desired, and leave to set. The icing will lose its shine over time.

MAKING TIME 15 MINUTES
BAKING TIME 35 MINUTES

MOCHA GÂTEAU

This cake is always very popular with young and old alike.

SERVES 8

- 1½ cups (6 oz/175g) self-rising flour
- ½ cup plus 2 tbsp (6 oz/175g) superfine sugar
- 12 tbsp (6 oz/170g) margarine, from fridge
- 3 large eggs
- 1 tbsp coffee extract
- ¾ level tsp baking powder

For the icing

- ½ cup (4 oz/114g) butter, softened
- 2 cups (8 oz/225g) confectioners' sugar, sifted
- 1½ tbsp coffee extract
- 5 tbsp (1½ oz/40g) drinking chocolate
- bittersweet or semisweet chocolate shavings, to decorate

1 Preheat the oven to 350°F/Convection 320°F. Grease two 8 in round sandwich tins and line the bases with nonstick baking paper.

2 Measure the cake ingredients into a large bowl and beat with an electric mixer until well blended.

3 Divide the mixture between the tins, level out evenly and bake in the preheated oven for about 35 minutes, or until the cakes are well risen and have shrunk slightly away from the sides of the tins.

4 Turn out, remove the paper and cool completely on a wire rack.

5 To make the icing, measure the butter, confectioners' sugar, coffee extract and drinking chocolate into a bowl and beat until smooth and well blended. Use half to sandwich the cakes together and the remainder to cover the top. Mark the cake attractively with a fork or round-bladed knife and then decorate with chocolate shavings.

MAKING TIME 20 MINUTES
BAKING TIME 20–25 MINUTES

CHOCOLATE BUTTON CAKE

A fabulous chocolate cake that is quick to make. Store in the fridge.

SERVES 8

- 2 level tbsp cocoa powder
- 2 tbsp hot water
- 12 tbsp (6 oz/170g) margarine, from fridge
- ½ cup plus 2 tbsp superfine sugar
- 3 large eggs
- 1½ cups (6 oz/175g) self-rising flour
- 1 level tsp baking powder
- a few drops peppermint extract

For the filling and topping

- 1¼ cups (10 oz/300ml) heavy cream, whipped
- 1 x 4½ oz (119g) package giant chocolate buttons, to decorate

1 Preheat the oven to 350°F/Convection 320°F. Grease two 8 in round sandwich tins and line the bases with nonstick baking paper.

2 Measure the cocoa and water into a large bowl and mix to a smooth paste. Add the remaining ingredients and beat well with an electric mixer until well blended.

3 Divide the mixture between the tins, level out evenly and bake in the preheated oven for 20–25 minutes, or until well risen and springing back when lightly pressed with a finger.

4 Leave to cool in the tins for about 5 minutes, then turn out, remove the paper and finish cooling on a wire rack.

5 Sandwich the cakes together with half the whipped cream and spread the remaining cream on top. Decorate with chocolate buttons.

MAKING TIME 5 MINUTES
BAKING TIME 45 MINUTES

CHOCOLATE ORANGE CAKE

This lovely moist cake is made in one bowl.

SERVES 6–8

- 1 cup (4 oz/125g) self-rising flour
- 2 tbsp (½ oz/15g) cocoa powder
- ½ level tsp baking powder
- ½ cup (4 oz/114g) margarine, from fridge
- ⅓ cup (3 oz/75g) superfine sugar
- 1 tbsp golden syrup (available online)
- 2 large eggs
- 2 oz (50g) bittersweet or semisweet chocolate, grated
- finely grated zest and juice of 1 orange

1 Preheat the oven to 320°F/Convection 270°F. Grease a 7 in round cake tin and line with nonstick baking paper.

2 Measure all the ingredients into a large bowl and beat with an electric mixer until well blended.

3 Turn the mixture into the tin, level the top and bake in the preheated oven for about 45 minutes, or until well risen, has shrunk slightly from the sides of the tin and the top springs back when lightly pressed with your fingertips.

4 Turn out and cool completely on a wire rack.

MAKING TIME 20 MINUTES
BAKING TIME 25–30 MINUTES

DEVIL'S FOOD CAKE

This is my version of the traditional American recipe; the yogurt gives a lovely texture.

SERVES 8

1 cup (8 oz/225g) superfine sugar
½ cup (2 oz/50g) cocoa powder, sifted
½ cup (5.5 oz/150g) plain yogurt
½ cup (4 oz/114g) margarine, from fridge
4 large eggs
2 cups (8 oz/225g) self-rising flour
1 level tsp baking powder

For the filling and topping

6 tbsp (3 oz/85g) butter, softened
1¼ cups (6 oz/175g) confectioners' sugar, sifted
3 oz (75g) bittersweet or semisweet chocolate, melted and cooled
apricot jam

1 Preheat the oven to 375°F/Convection 325°F. Grease two 8 in round sandwich tins and line the bases with nonstick baking paper.

2 Measure all the ingredients for the cake into a large bowl and beat with an electric mixer until well blended and smooth.

3 Divide the mixture between the tins, level out evenly and bake in the preheated oven for 25–30 minutes, or until well risen, shrinking away from the sides of the tins and the tops spring back when lightly pressed with your fingertips.

4 Leave to cool in the tins for a few minutes then turn out, remove the paper and finish cooling on a wire rack.

5 To make the icing, cream the butter with the confectioners' sugar until light and fluffy, then stir in the melted chocolate.

6 Sandwich the sponges together with a layer of apricot jam and half the icing. Spread the remaining icing on top. Decorate the cake by drawing squiggly lines in the icing with a fork.

MAKING TIME 25 MINUTES
BAKING TIME 20 MINUTES

CHOCOLATE CUPCAKES

These are delicious topped with a fresh raspberry but would look lovely with a nasturtium flower, too.

MAKES 12

- 10 tbsp (5 oz/140g) margarine, from fridge
- ½ cup plus 1 tbsp (5 oz/150g) superfine sugar
- 1 cup (4½ oz/115g) self-rising flour
- 5 tbsp (1¼ oz/35g) cocoa powder
- 3 large eggs
- 1 level tsp baking powder
- a handful of fresh raspberries, to decorate (optional)

For the icing

- 4 oz (100g) bittersweet or semisweet chocolate, broken into pieces
- 4 tbsp water
- 2 tbsp (1 oz/30g) butter
- 1¼ cups (6 oz/175g) confectioners' sugar, sifted

1 Preheat the oven to 400°F/Convection 350°F and arrange 12 paper liners in a muffin tin.

2 Measure all the ingredients for the cakes except the raspberries into a large bowl and beat with an electric mixer until well blended and smooth.

3 Divide the mixture among the muffin cups and bake in the preheated oven for about 20 minutes, or until the cakes are well risen and spring back when lightly pressed with a finger.

4 Remove from the oven and cool completely on a wire rack.

5 For the icing, measure the chocolate, water and butter into a heatproof bowl and heat gently over a pan of simmering water until the chocolate and butter have melted. Remove from the heat, beat until smooth, then stir in the confectioners' sugar until thoroughly mixed.

6 Leave to cool until just beginning to set, then spread a little on the top of each cake. If desired, top each cake with a raspberry, or other fruit in season, before serving.

MAKING TIME 10 MINUTES
CHILLING TIME 6 HOURS

NO-BAKE CHOCOLATE JULIETTE

This chocolate loaf is very rich, so serve it in thin slices—and offer pastry forks to your guests.

SERVES 8–10

- ½ cup plus 6 tbsp (7 oz/200g) butter
- 8 oz (225g) bittersweet or semisweet chocolate, broken into pieces
- 2 tbsp rum or brandy
- 6 oz (175g) Nice biscuits or other coconut-flavored shortbread

1 Line a small 8½ × 4½ in (1 lb) loaf tin with plastic wrap.

2 Measure the butter and chocolate into a heatproof bowl. Place the bowl on top of a pan of boiling water and heat gently until the mixture has melted and is smooth and runny. Stir in the rum or brandy.

3 Break the biscuits into ½ in pieces and stir into the chocolate mixture.

4 Pack the chocolate mixture into the tin and smooth the top with the back of a spoon.

5 Leave to chill in the fridge for about 6 hours, until set.

6 Turn out onto a serving plate and peel off the plastic wrap. Cut into 8–10 slices to serve.

MAKING TIME 30 MINUTES
CHILLING TIME 6 HOURS

MOCHA BRANDY GÂTEAU

You will enjoy both making and eating this. If you have a deep loaf tin, rather than a long, shallow one, you may need a few more sponge fingers to line it.

SERVES 6–8

- 4 tbsp brandy
- 1 level tbsp instant coffee granules
- 6 tbsp boiling water
- 10 sponge fingers, each one halved widthwise
- cocoa powder, to dust (optional)
- bittersweet or semisweet chocolate shavings, to decorate (optional)

For the filling

- 2¼ tbsp (2 oz/50g) superfine sugar
- 6 tbsp water
- 4 oz (100g) bittersweet or semisweet chocolate, chopped into small pieces
- 2 large egg yolks, beaten
- 1¼ cups (10 oz/300ml) heavy cream

1 Wet the inside of a 9 × 5 in (2 lb) loaf tin and line with plastic wrap.

2 Measure the brandy, coffee and boiling water into a heatproof bowl. Mix well, then quickly dip the sponge fingers into the liquid. Line the sides and edges of the tin with the sponges.

3 To make the filling, measure the sugar and water into a saucepan and dissolve the sugar slowly over a low heat. Increase the heat and bring to the boil. Boil for a few seconds until you have a thin syrup.

4 Remove from the heat and add the chocolate. Stir until completely melted.

5 Add the egg yolks and mix well.

6 Lightly whip the double cream in a large bowl. Fold in the chocolate mixture and mix until smooth.

7 Pour into the tin and level the top. Cover with plastic film and leave to chill in the fridge for about 6 hours, or until set.

8 Remove the plastic wrap from the top of the loaf tin, turn upside down on to a serving plate and remove the tin and remaining plastic wrap. Dust with cocoa powder and decorate with chocolate shavings, if liked.

9 Cut into 6–8 slices to serve.

MAKING TIME 25 MINUTES
BAKING TIME 25–30 MINUTES

MILLIONAIRE'S SHORTBREAD

These are not ultra-quick to make but are great favorites with all ages. Do not expect the caramel to harden—it doesn't. The shortbread is gooey and sticky to eat.

MAKES 21

For the base
½ cup (4 oz/114g) butter, softened
2¼ tbsp (2 oz/50g) superfine sugar
1¼ cups (5 oz/15g) all-purpose flour

For the caramel
½ cup (4 oz/114g) butter
3 tbsp (3 oz/75g) superfine sugar
2 tbsp golden syrup (available online)
½ x 14 oz (397g) can condensed milk

For the topping
4 oz (100g) bittersweet or semisweet chocolate, broken into pieces

1 Preheat the oven to 350°F/Convection 320°F and grease an 11 x 7 in baking tin.

2 Place all the ingredients for the base in a bowl and beat to a firm dough. (The mixture may require a light kneading with the hand to come together.)

3 Press into the tin with the back of a spoon. Prick with a fork then bake in the preheated oven for 25–30 minutes, until a pale brown.

4 While the shortbread is baking, prepare the caramel. Measure all the ingredients into a saucepan and heat gently until melted. Bring the mixture to a boil and leave to bubble for 10–15 minutes until it is caramel colored. Stir continuously, preferably with a flat-based wooden spoon that can get into the sides of the pan and prevent the mixture from catching.

5 Remove from the heat and leave to cool slightly.

6 When the shortbread is cooked and has cooled for about 5 minutes, pour the caramel over the top and set aside.

7 Break the chocolate into pieces and place in a small heatproof bowl set over a saucepan of water. Heat gently until the chocolate has melted and is smooth.

8 Pour the chocolate in a steady stream over the caramel to make a thin layer of chocolate on top. Before the chocolate has hardened, drag a fork gently through it to make swirling patterns. Leave to set.

9 Cut into 21 pieces to serve.

MAKING TIME 15 MINUTES
BAKING TIME 20 MINUTES

CHOCOLATE ÉCLAIRS

Everybody's favorite. Be sure to dry out the pastry cases thoroughly after baking before filling with cream, so that they are crisp to eat. Ideally, the éclairs should be filled just before serving so that they retain this crispiness.

MAKES 20

¼ cup (2 oz/55g) butter
¾ cup (6 oz/150ml) water
½ cup (2 oz/65g) bread flour
2 large eggs, beaten

For the filling

1¼ cups (10 oz/300ml) heavy cream, whipped

For the icing

2 cups (8 oz/225g) confectioners' sugar
1 level tbsp cocoa powder
1 tbsp rum
1–2 tbsp warm water

1 Preheat the oven to 400°F/Convection 350°F and grease two large baking sheets.

2 Put the butter and water in a saucepan and bring to the boil, stirring occasionally. Remove from the heat and add the flour all at once and beat until the mixture forms a ball. Leave to cool slightly then gradually beat in the eggs to make a smooth, shiny paste.

3 Place the mixture in a piping bag fitted with a ½ in plain pipe. Pipe 20 éclairs, each about 2 in long, onto the baking sheets, leaving room for them to expand during cooking. Bake in the preheated oven for about 20 minutes, or until well risen and golden brown.

4 Remove from the oven and split one side of each éclair with a knife to allow the steam to escape. Leave to cool on a wire rack. If the insides of the split éclairs are still moist, return them to the oven to dry out for 5 minutes more.

5 Pipe or spoon the whipped cream into the middle of the base of the éclairs and replace the top.

6 To make the icing, sift the confectioners' sugar and cocoa into a bowl and stir in the rum and just sufficient warm water to make a thick icing. Spear each éclair with a fork and dip the tops in the icing. Leave to set, and serve on the day they are made and filled.

MAKING TIME 30 MINUTES
BAKING TIME 20 MINUTES

COFFEE AND CHOCOLATE ÉCLAIRS

These are one of my most favorite things to eat. The coffee filling makes them that little bit more special.

MAKES 20

4 tbsp (2 oz/55g) butter
¾ cup (6 oz/150ml) water
½ cup (2 oz/65g) bread flour
2 large eggs, beaten

For the filling

½ cup (2 oz/50g) confectioners' sugar, sifted
1 tbsp coffee extract
1¼ cups (10 oz/300ml) heavy cream, whipped

For the icing

2 oz (50g) bittersweet or semisweet chocolate, broken into pieces
2 tbsp water
1 tbsp butter
¾ cup (3 oz/75g) confectioners' sugar, sifted

1 Preheat the oven to 400°F/Convection 350°F and grease two large baking sheets.

2 Put the butter and water in a saucepan and bring to the boil, stirring occasionally. Remove from the heat and add the flour all at once and beat until the mixture forms a ball. Leave to cool slightly then gradually beat in the eggs to make a smooth, shiny paste.

3 Place the mixture in a piping bag fitted with a ½ in plain pipe. Pipe 20 éclairs, each about 2 in long, onto the baking sheets, leaving room for them to expand during cooking. Bake in the preheated oven for about 20 minutes, or until well risen and golden brown.

4 Remove from the oven and split one side of each éclair with a knife to allow the steam to escape. Leave to cool on a wire rack. If the insides of the split éclairs are still moist, return them to the oven to dry out for 5 minutes more.

5 To make the filling, fold the confectioners' sugar and coffee extract into the whipped cream. Pipe or spoon the cream into the middle of the base of the éclairs and replace the top.

6 To make the icing, measure the chocolate, water and butter into a heatproof bowl and heat gently over a pan of simmering water until melted. Remove from the heat and beat in the confectioners' sugar until smooth. Pour into a shallow dish and dip each éclair into the chocolate mixture to coat the top. Leave to set, and serve on the day they are made and filled.

MAKING TIME 10 MINUTES
BAKING TIME 35–40 MINUTES

RICH CHOCOLATE TRAYBAKE

Ideally you should ice the cake in the tin and, when set, lift out with an offset spatula.

MAKES 16 PIECES

3 level tbsp cocoa powder, sifted
3 tbsp hot water
1 cup (8 oz/225g) margarine, from fridge
1 cup (8 oz/225g) superfine sugar
2¼ cups (10 oz/275g) self-rising flour
1 level tsp baking powder
4 large eggs

For the icing

6 tbsp (3 oz/85g) butter, softened
½ cup (2 oz/50g) cocoa powder, sifted
2 cups (8 oz/225g) confectioners' sugar, sifted
2 tbsp milk

1 Preheat the oven to 350°F/Convection 320°F. Grease a 12 x 9 in traybake tin and line with nonstick baking paper.

2 Blend the cocoa for the cake with the hot water in a large bowl and leave to cool slightly. Measure all the rest of the cake ingredients into the bowl and beat with an electric mixer until well blended and smooth.

3 Turn the mixture into the tin and level the top. Bake in the preheated oven for 35–40 minutes, or until the cake has shrunk a little from the sides of the tin and springs back when pressed in the center with your fingertips.

4 Cool completely in the tin.

5 To make the icing, measure all the ingredients into a large bowl and beat well until the icing has thickened. Spread the icing all over the traybake and leave to set.

6 Cut into 16 pieces to serve.

MAKING TIME 10 MINUTES
BAKING TIME 30–35 MINUTES

WHITE CHOCOLATE AND STRAWBERRY TRAYBAKE

When you buy freeze-dried strawberries from a supermarket, they come in 2 oz (56g) tubes. Use half for the cake and half for the topping.

MAKES 20 PIECES

- 1 cup (8 oz/225g) margarine, from fridge
- 1 cup (8 oz/225g) superfine sugar
- 2½ cups (10 oz/275g) self-rising flour
- 1 level tsp baking powder
- 4 large eggs
- 4 tbsp milk
- 1 tsp vanilla extract
- ¼ x 2 oz (56g) tube freeze-dried strawberries, chopped
- 4 oz (100g) white chocolate, melted

For the topping

- ½ cup (4 oz/114g) butter, softened
- 1½ cups (6 oz/175g) confectioners' sugar, sifted
- 2 tbsp milk
- ½ tsp vanilla extract
- ¼ x 2 oz (56g) tube freeze-dried strawberries, chopped

1 Preheat the oven to 350°F/Convection 320°F. Grease a 12 x 9 in traybake tin and line with nonstick baking paper.

2 Measure all the traybake ingredients, except the strawberries and white chocolate, into a large bowl and beat with an electric mixer until light and fluffy. Stir in the strawberries and melted chocolate.

3 Turn the mixture into the tin and level the top. Bake in the preheated oven for 30–35 minutes, or until the cake has shrunk a little from the sides of the tin and springs back when pressed in the center with your fingertips.

4 Cool completely in the tin.

5 To make the icing, measure the butter, confectioners' sugar, milk and vanilla into a bowl. Whisk until pale and creamy. Spread over the traybake and sprinkle with the strawberries.

MAKING TIME 15 MINUTES
BAKING TIME 10–12 MINUTES

TOLL HOUSE COOKIES

These biscuits are very easy to make and the children love finding the pieces of chocolate in them.

MAKES ABOUT 20

- ½ cup (4 oz/114g) butter, softened
- ½ cup (4 oz/100g) light muscovado sugar
- 1 large egg
- 1 tsp vanilla extract
- 1¼ cup plus 2 tbsp (5 oz/150g) all-purpose flour
- 1 level tsp baking powder
- ½ cup (4 oz/100g) semisweet chocolate chips

1 Preheat the oven to 375°F/Convection 325°F and line two or three baking sheets with nonstick baking paper.

2 Measure the butter and sugar into a bowl and beat well until soft and creamy. Work in all the remaining ingredients until the mixture forms a stiff dough.

3 Divide the mixture into small pieces. Put these on the baking sheets then press flat with the palm of your hand. Bake in the preheated oven for 10–12 minutes, until they are golden brown.

4 Leave to cool on the baking sheets for a few moments, then lift off using an offset spatula and finish cooling on a wire rack.

MAKING TIME 15 MINUTES
BAKING TIME 10 MINUTES

CHOCOLATE BISCUITS

Lovely, light crunchy cookies that keep well in an airtight container.

MAKES 20

½ cup (4 oz/114g) butter, softened
4½ tbsp (2 oz/50g) superfine sugar
1¼ cups (5 oz/150g) self-rising flour
5 tbsp (1 oz/25g) cocoa powder

1 Preheat the oven to 375°F/Convection 325°F and line two large baking sheets with nonstick baking paper.

2 Measure the butter and sugar into a bowl and cream together until light. Work in the flour and cocoa. (This is done most easily by kneading the mixture together with your hands until smooth.)

3 Take heaped teaspoonfuls of the mixture and roll it into small balls. Arrange on the prepared baking sheets, flatten down with a fork that has been dipped in cold water and bake in the preheated oven for about 10 minutes.

4 Leave to cool on the baking sheets for a few moments, then lift off using an offset spatula and finish cooling on a wire rack.

MAKING TIME 20 MINUTES
BAKING TIME 15–20 MINUTES

CHOCOLATE CREAM FINGERS

These are very similar to a well-known biscuit that is sold in shops; my family think these are far nicer and are always asking me to make them. Rolling the dough between plastic wrap makes it easy to handle.

MAKES 10–12

For the biscuits

- 1 cup (4 oz/100g) all-purpose flour
- ½ level tsp baking powder
- 2 level tbsp cocoa powder
- 4 tbsp (2 oz/55g) butter, softened
- 4½ tbsp (2 oz/50g) superfine sugar
- 1 tbsp golden syrup (available online)
- 2 tsp milk

For the filling

- 2 tbsp (1 oz/30g) butter, softened
- ½ cup (2 oz/50g) confectioners' sugar, sifted
- 2 level tsp cocoa powder
- a few drops vanilla extract
- 1 tsp milk

1 Place all the biscuit ingredients together in a bowl and beat well until they are blended and smooth. Bring the mixture together using your hands. Cover and chill in the fridge for 30 minutes.

2 Preheat the oven to 320°F/Convection 270°F and line two large baking sheets with nonstick baking paper.

3 Place a sheet of plastic wrap on a work surface and place the dough on top. Place another sheet of plastic wrap over the dough and roll out to about ¼ in thickness. Remove the top sheet of plastic wrap and cut the dough into fingers about 1 in wide and about 2½ in long. You should get 20–24 fingers from the dough.

4 Carefully lift each finger onto a baking sheet and prick each biscuit two or three times with a fork. Bake in the preheated oven for 15–20 minutes.

5 Leave to cool on the sheets for a few moments, then lift off with an offset spatula and finish cooling on a wire rack.

6 To make the filling, measure all the ingredients into a bowl and beat well until smooth and creamy. Use to sandwich the biscuits together in pairs.

MAKING TIME 15 MINUTES
CHILLING TIME 1 HOUR

BOOZY RUM TRUFFLES

This is a good way of using up broken biscuits and, perhaps, a stale sponge. The truffles are quick to make and require no cooking. Add trimmings of icing or marzipan, if you have them left after icing the Christmas cake. Make this recipe in two batches and keep the truffles in the fridge or store in the freezer until required.

MAKES 35–40

- 2–3 tbsp rum
- ½ cup (4 oz/100g) seedless raisins, finely chopped
- 4 tbsp apricot jam, warmed
- 5 oz (150g) broken plain biscuits, such as Viennese Finger Biscuits on page 206, crushed
- 7 oz (200g) Madeira or sponge cake, crumbled
- 4 oz (100g) bittersweet or semisweet chocolate, melted
- 4 oz (110g) chocolate sprinkles

1 Arrange about 40 petit four cups on a baking sheet.

2 Measure the rum, raisins, jam, biscuits and cake into a large bowl. Add the melted chocolate and mix together very thoroughly until the mixture is evenly covered in chocolate.

3 Shape into about 40 little balls and roll each one in the chocolate sprinkles. Place in the petit four cups.

4 Leave the truffles to chill in the fridge for about 1 hour before eating.

CHAPTER FOUR

FAMILY FRUIT CAKES

MAKING TIME 15 MINUTES
BAKING TIME 1¼ HOURS

EASY APPLE CAKE

It is best to use a loose-bottomed cake or springform tin for this as it is often difficult to turn out. If you do not have one, line the base of an ordinary tin with foil or baking paper and, after allowing it to cool for 15 minutes, carefully turn out onto a flat plate. Then peel off the foil or paper and reverse the cake onto another plate.

SERVES 8

- 9 oz (250g) cooking apples (peeled weight)
- 1¼ cups (6 oz/175g) self-rising flour
- ¾ cup (6 oz/175g) superfine sugar, plus extra to sprinkle
- 2 large eggs
- ½ tsp almond extract
- ½ cup (4 oz/120ml) heavy cream, for serving butter, melted

1 Preheat the oven to 350°F/Convection 320°F and line an 8 in loose-bottomed cake or springform tin with nonstick baking paper.

2 Core and thinly slice the apples and put them in a bowl of water.

3 Measure the flour into a bowl with the sugar. Beat the eggs and almond extract together and stir them into the flour, together with the melted butter, and mix well. Spread half of the mixture into the tin.

4 Drain and dry the apples with paper towels and arrange them on the cake mixture. Top with the remaining batter; it is not very easy to spread, but if the apples show through it doesn't matter too much.

5 Bake in the preheated oven for 1¼ hours, or until golden and shrinking slightly from the sides of the tin.

6 Leave to cool for 15 minutes, then turn out and remove the paper.

7 Sift over some sugar and serve warm with cream.

VARIATION: MINI APPLE CAKES

Prepare the cake mix and apples as above. Arrange 12 paper liners in a muffin tin. Place 1 tablespoon of the cake mix in each muffin liners and top with the sliced apples. Cover with the remaining cake batter and bake in the preheated oven for 25–30 minutes until well risen and lightly brown.

MAKING TIME 10 MINUTES
BAKING TIME 1½ HOURS

SPECIAL APRICOT CAKE

Utterly delicious. A can of apricots is added to this cake and gives it its distinctive flavor. Use the juice from the can in a fruit salad or soak sponge cakes in it for a trifle. I've added a small bake version—these are lovely served warm.

SERVES 6–8

- ½ cup (4 oz/115g) margarine, from fridge
- ½ cup (4 oz/100g) light muscovado sugar
- 2 large eggs
- ¼ tsp almond extract
- 1¾ cups (7 oz/200g) self-rising flour
- ½ level tsp baking powder
- ½ x 15 oz (425g) can apricot halves, drained and chopped
- 1 cup (7 oz/200g) mixed dried fruit

1 Preheat the oven to 320°F/Convection 270°F. Grease a 7 in round cake tin and line with nonstick baking paper.

2 Measure all the ingredients except the fruit into a large mixing bowl and beat with an electric mixer until well blended. Stir in the apricots and dried fruit.

3 Turn the mixture into the tin and level the top. Bake in the preheated oven for 1½ hours, or until the cake is golden brown. A skewer inserted into the center of the cake should come out clean.

4 Leave to cool in the tin for 10 minutes then turn out, remove the paper and leave to cool on a wire rack.

VARIATION: MINI APRICOT CAKES

Prepare the cake mix as above and use to fill 12 paper liners set in a muffin tin. Cook for 25–30 minutes at 350°F/Convection 320°F until well risen and lightly brown. Serve warm.

MAKING TIME 10–15 MINUTES
BAKING TIME 25 MINUTES

PINEAPPLE UPSIDE-DOWN CAKE

This cake always looks and tastes good and is delicious if served warm at a coffee morning.

SERVES 6–8

For the cake
¾ cup (3 oz/75g) self-rising flour
6 tbsp (3 oz/85g) margarine, from fridge
⅔ cup (3 oz/75g) superfine sugar
1 large egg, beaten
1 tbsp pineapple juice

For the topping
¼ cup (2 oz/50g) light muscovado sugar
1 x 8 oz (227g) can pineapple slices, drained
2 glacé cherries, halved

1 Preheat the oven to 375°F/Convection 325°F and thoroughly grease a 7 in round cake tin (don't use a tin with a removable base or the syrup will leak through).

2 Measure all the cake ingredients into a bowl and beat with an electric mixer until well blended.

3 Sprinkle the brown sugar in the bottom of the tin and place 4 pineapple rings on top. Add a halved cherry in the center of each ring, then carefully spread the cake mixture over the pineapples and level the top.

4 Bake in the preheated oven for about 25 minutes, or until well risen and golden brown and the center springs back when lightly pressed with your fingertips.

5 Leave to cool for about 20 minutes in the tin, then turn out onto a serving plate.

MAKING TIME 15 MINUTES
BAKING TIME 2 HOURS

PINEAPPLE AND RAISIN CAKE

This is a less rich, moist kind of Christmas cake. It is best made just before Christmas, kept cool and eaten within a month—store in a plastic container in the fridge. Drain the pineapple very well and keep the juice for a fruit salad or trifle. I've added a small bake version for when you want a quick fruity cupcake.

SERVES 8

- 1 x 8 oz (227g) can pineapple (chunks, rings or crushed), excluding the juice
- 10 tbsp (5 oz/140g) butter, softened
- ½ cup (4 oz/100g) light muscovado sugar
- 2 large eggs
- 1¾ cups (7 oz/200g) self-rising flour
- 2 tbsp milk
- 2¼ cups (14 oz/400g) seedless raisins

1 Preheat the oven to 320°F/Convection 270°F. Grease an 8 in round cake tin and line with nonstick baking paper.

2 Drain and chop the pineapple very finely, then dry with paper towels.

3 Cream the butter and sugar together in a bowl using an electric mixer. Beat in the eggs, adding a tablespoon of flour with the last egg. Fold in the flour and stir in the milk and, last of all, the fruit, including the pineapple.

4 Turn into the tin, place in the center of the preheated oven and bake for about 2 hours, or until the cake is a pale golden brown and shrinking away from the sides of the tin.

5 Leave to cool in the tin then remove the paper to serve or store in an airtight container.

VARIATION: MINI PINEAPPLE AND RAISIN CAKES

Preheat the oven to 350°F/Convection 320°F. and arrange 12 paper liners in a muffin tin. Using 8 oz (225g) of raisins instead of 14 oz (400g), measure all the ingredients into a large mixing bowl and beat with an electric mixer until well blended. Spoon into the muffin cups and bake for 25–30 minutes, or until well risen and lightly brown. Serve warm.

MAKING TIME 15 MINUTES
BAKING TIME 1¼ HOURS

SPECIAL CHERRY CAKE

A classic cake. It is important to cut the cherries up and then wash and dry them thoroughly so that all moisture is removed.

SERVES 8

- 6 oz (175g) glacé cherries
- 2 cups (8 oz/225g) self-rising flour
- 12 tbsp (6 oz/170g) margarine, from fridge
- ¾ cup (6 oz/175g) superfine sugar
- finely grated zest of 1 lemon
- ½ cup (2 oz/50g) almond flour
- 3 large eggs

1 Preheat the oven to 320°F/Convection 270°F. Grease an 8 in round cake tin and line with nonstick baking paper.

2 Cut each cherry into quarters, put in a sieve and rinse under running water. Drain well and dry very thoroughly with paper towels.

3 Place all the remaining ingredients in a large bowl and beat with an electric mixer until well blended. Lightly fold in the cherries. The mixture will be fairly stiff, which will help to keep the cherries evenly suspended in the cake while it bakes.

4 Turn into the tin and bake in the preheated oven for about 1¼ hours, or until a skewer inserted into the center of the cake comes out clean.

5 Leave to cool in the tin for 10 minutes, then turn out and finish cooling on a wire rack.

6 Store in an airtight container.

MAKING TIME 10 MINUTES
BAKING TIME 1¾ HOURS

MINCEMEAT CAKE

This is a very light, moist fruit cake and is quite delicious. This small bake version takes only 25–30 minutes in the oven and would make a lovely alternative to Christmas cake in the festive season.

SERVES 10

- 10 tbsp (5 oz/140g) margarine, from fridge
- ½ cup plus 1 tbsp (5 oz/150g) light muscovado sugar
- 2 large eggs
- 2 cups (8 oz/225g) self-rising flour
- ½ cup (3 oz/75g) sultanas
- 1 cup (8 oz/225g) mincemeat
- ¼ cup (1 oz/25g) slivered almonds

1 Preheat the oven to 320°F/Convection 270°F. Grease an 8 in round cake tin and line with nonstick baking paper.

2 Measure the margarine, sugar, eggs and flour into a large bowl and beat with an electric mixer until well blended. Stir in the sultanas and mincemeat.

3 Turn the mixture into the tin, level the top and sprinkle over the almonds. Bake in the preheated oven for about 1¾ hours, or until golden brown and shrinking away from the sides of the tin.

4 Cool completely in the tin, then remove the paper to serve or store in an airtight container.

VARIATION: MINI MINCEMEAT CAKES

Preheat the oven to 350°F/Convection 320°F and arrange 12 paper liners in a muffin tin. Using 6 oz (175g) of mincemeat instead of 8 oz (225g), measure all the ingredients, except the almonds, into a large mixing bowl and beat with a wooden spoon until well blended. Spoon into the liners, sprinkle with the slivered almonds and bake for 25–30 minutes, or until well risen and lightly brown. Cool on a wire rack.

MAKING TIME 10 MINUTES
BAKING TIME 1 HOUR

FRUGAL CAKE

A basic and easy family fruit cake that can be made with any dried fruit you have in the cupboard. It's best eaten on the day it is made.

SERVES 8

- 2 cups (8 oz/225g) self-rising flour
- ½ cup (4 oz/114g) margarine, from fridge
- ½ cup (4 oz/100g) light muscovado sugar
- 2 large eggs
- 3 tbsp milk
- 1¾ cups (8 oz/225g) mixed dried fruit
- 1 level tbsp demerara sugar

1 Preheat the oven to 350°F/Convection 320°F. Grease a 7 in deep round cake tin and line with nonstick baking paper.

2 Measure all the ingredients, except the dried fruit and demerara sugar, into a large mixing bowl and beat with an electric mixer until well blended. Stir in the dried fruit.

3 Turn the mixture into the tin, level the top and sprinkle with the demerara sugar. Bake in the preheated oven for about 1 hour, or until a skewer inserted into the center of the cake comes out clean.

4 Leave to cool in the tin for about 30 minutes, then turn out, remove the paper and finish cooling on a wire rack.

MAKING TIME 10 MINUTES
BAKING TIME 25–30 MINUTES

BANANA AND CHOCOLATE CHIP MUFFINS

Banana and chocolate is a great combination and these American-style muffins are popular with children. They are also very easy to make.

MAKES 12

2 ripe bananas, mashed with a fork
2¼ cups (9 oz/250g) self-rising flour
1 level tsp baking powder
½ cup (4 oz/114g) margarine, from fridge
¾ cup (6 oz/175g) light muscovado sugar
2 large eggs
½ cup (5½ oz/150g) plain yogurt
2 tbsp milk
½ cup (4 oz/100g) dark chocolate chips

1 Preheat the oven to 350°F/Convection 320°F and arrange 12 paper liners in a muffin tin.

2 Measure all the ingredients except the chocolate chips into a large bowl and beat with an electric mixer until well blended. Stir in the chocolate chips.

3 Spoon into the liners and bake in the preheated oven for 25–30 minutes, until well risen and lightly golden brown.

4 Lift off and cool completely on a wire rack.

MAKING TIME 15 MINUTES
BAKING TIME 25 MINUTES

MINI FRUIT CUPCAKES

If you don't have time to bake a fruit cake, try this recipe. Here I've taken the basic fruit cake mix and turned it into a really quick bake.

MAKES 12

½ cup (4 oz/114g) butter, softened
½ cup (4 oz/100g) superfine sugar
finely grated zest of 1 small orange
2 large eggs
½ level tsp ground ginger
1 cup (4 oz/100g) self-rising flour
1½ cups (6 oz/175g) mixed dried fruit
1 oz (25g) glacé cherries, chopped, rinsed and thoroughly dried

1 Preheat the oven to 350°F/Convection 320°F and arrange 12 paper liners in a muffin tin.

2 Measure all the ingredients except the mixed fruit and cherries, into a large bowl and beat with an electric mixer until light, fluffy and well blended. Stir in the fruit and cherries.

3 Spoon into the liners and bake in the preheated oven for about 25 minutes, or until well risen and lightly golden brown.

4 Cool on a wire rack.

MAKING TIME 25 MINUTES
BAKING TIME 1¾–2 HOURS

VICARAGE FRUIT CAKE

This cake keeps very well if you wrap it in foil or store it in an airtight container. It is a moist fruit cake and is ideal to cut and include in a lunch box or to take on a picnic.

SERVES 8

- 1 x 14 oz (396g) can full-fat condensed milk
- 10 tbsp (5 oz/140g) margarine, from fridge
- 1¾ cups (8 oz/225g) seedless raisins
- 1¾ cups (8 oz/225g) sultanas
- 1¾ cups (8 oz/225g) currants
- 4 oz (100g) glacé cherries, chopped, rinsed and thoroughly dried
- 2 cups (8 oz/225g) all-purpose flour
- 2 level tsp pumpkin pie spice
- 1 level tsp ground cinnamon
- ½ level tsp baking soda
- 2 large eggs

1 Preheat the oven to 300°F/Confection 250°F. Grease a 7 in round cake tin and line with nonstick baking paper.

2 Pour the condensed milk into a heavy-bottomed saucepan. Add the margarine, fruit and glacé cherries. Place over low heat until the spread has melted. Stir well and warm through for 5 minutes, stirring regularly so the condensed milk doesn't form a skin.

3 Remove from the heat and set aside to cool for about 10 minutes, stirring occasionally to help speed up the cooling.

4 Meanwhile, sift the flour, spices and baking soda into a large bowl and make a well in the center. Add the eggs and the cooled fruit mixture and mix together quickly until well blended.

5 Turn the mixture into the tin, level the top and bake in the preheated oven for 1¾–2 hours, or until well risen. A skewer inserted into the center of the cake should come out clean.

6 Leave to cool in the tin for about 10 minutes, then turn out and leave to finish cooling on a wire rack.

MAKING TIME 15 MINUTES
BAKING TIME 1½ HOURS

DUNDEE CAKE

All the better for keeping for a week or so.

SERVES 12

- 10 tbsp (5 oz/140g) butter, softened
- ½ cup plus 1 tbsp (5 oz/150g) light muscovado sugar
- 3 large eggs
- 2¼ cups (9 oz/250g) all-purpose flour
- 1 level tsp baking powder
- 1¼ cups (6 oz/175g) sultanas
- ½ cup (3 oz/75g) currants
- ½ cup (3 oz/75g) seedless raisins
- 2 oz (50g) glacé cherries, halved, rinsed and thoroughly dried
- 2 oz (50g) mixed candied citrus peel, chopped
- 2 level tbsp almond flour
- finely grated zest of 1 large lemon
- ⅔ cup (2 oz/50g) blanched almonds, halved, to decorate

1 Preheat the oven to 320°F/Convection 270°F. Grease an 8 in loose-bottomed cake or springform tin and line with nonstick baking paper.

2 Measure the butter, sugar, eggs, flour and baking powder into a large bowl and beat with an electric mixer until well blended. Stir in the fruit, peel, almond flour and lemon zest.

3 Spoon the mixture into the cake tin and smooth the top. Arrange the almonds in circles over the top of the cake and bake in the preheated oven for about 1½ hours, or until a deep golden brown. A warm skewer inserted into the center of the cake should come out clean. Cover the cake with foil halfway through baking if it is browning too quickly.

4 Leave to cool in the tin for about 20 minutes, then turn out, remove the paper and finish cooling on a wire rack.

MAKING TIME 15 MINUTES
BAKING TIME 2–2½ HOURS

FAMILY FRUIT CAKE

This cake improves with keeping and is the ideal cake to bake a week in advance and take with you when you've rented a house for vacation.

SERVES 10

- 1 cup (8 oz/225g) butter, softened
- 1 cup (8 oz/225g) superfine sugar
- finely grated zest of 1 orange
- 4 large eggs
- 1 level tsp ground ginger
- 2 cups (8 oz/225g) self-rising flour
- 2¼ cups (12 oz/350g) mixed dried fruit
- 2 oz (50g) glacé cherries, quartered, rinsed and thoroughly dried

1 Preheat the oven to 320°F/Convection 270°F. Grease a deep, 8 in round cake tin and line with nonstick baking paper.

2 Measure the butter, sugar, orange zest, eggs, ginger and flour into a large bowl. Beat with an electric mixer until light, fluffy and well blended. Stir in the mixed fruit and cherries.

3 Turn the mixture into the tin, level the top and bake in the preheated oven for 2–2½ hours, or until the middle feels firm to the touch. A skewer inserted into the center of the cake should come out clean.

4 Leave to cool in the tin, then remove the paper to store in an airtight container.

MAKING TIME 15 MINUTES
BAKING TIME 2¼ HOURS

EASTER SIMNEL CAKE

The traditional Easter cake.

SERVES 10

- 12 tbsp (6 oz/170g) margarine, from fridge
- ½ cup plus 2 tbsp (6 oz/175g) light muscovado sugar
- 3 large eggs
- 1½ cups (6 oz/175g) self-rising flour
- 2 level tsp pumpkin pie spice
- 2 tbsp milk
- 1¾ cups (10 oz/275g) mixed dried fruit
- 2 oz (50g) glacé cherries, halved, rinsed and thoroughly dried
- finely grated zest of 1 orange or lemon
- ½ cup (2 oz/50g) almond flour

For the decoration

- 1 lb (450g) golden marzipan
- 1 tbsp apricot jam, sieved
- 1 large egg white, beaten with a fork

1 Preheat the oven to 320°F/Convection 270°F. Grease a deep, 7 in round cake tin and line with nonstick baking paper.

2 Measure all the cake ingredients into a large bowl and beat together with a wooden spoon until well blended—this will take 2–3 minutes.

3 Place half the cake mixture in the bottom of the tin and level the top.

4 Take one-third of the marzipan and roll out to a circle the size of the tin, then place on top of the cake mixture. Cover with the remaining cake mixture and level the top.

5 Bake in the preheated oven for about 2¼ hours, or until a skewer inserted into the center of the cake comes out clean.

6 Turn out, remove the paper and leave to cool on a wire rack.

7 Brush the top of the cooled cake with the jam then roll half the remaining marzipan into a circle to fit the top of the cake. Press in place and pinch the edges to crimp decoratively.

8 Roll out the remaining marzipan and shape into 11 small balls. Arrange the balls around the edge of the cake. Using a sharp knife, score the center of the marzipan in a crisscross pattern. Brush with a little egg white and put under a preheated broiler for 3–4 minutes to brown lightly. Leave to cool.

SOAKING TIME 3 DAYS
MAKING TIME 10 MINUTES
BAKING TIME 4–4½ HOURS

VICTORIAN CHRISTMAS CAKE

An easy and special Christmas cake. The fruit is soaked for three days, which makes it very moist. This is not a deep cake so don't expect it to rise to the top of the tin.

SERVES 12

- 1⅛ cups (6 oz/175g) seedless raisins, chopped
- 3 cups (1lb 2 oz/500g) currants
- 2⅓ cups (12 oz/350g) sultanas
- 2⅓ cups (12 oz/350g) glacé cherries, quartered, rinsed and thoroughly dried
- ¾ cup (6 oz/150ml) medium sherry
- finely grated zest of 2 oranges
- 1 cup plus 1 tbsp (9 oz/250g) butter, softened
- 1 cup plus 1 tbsp (9 oz/250g) muscovado sugar
- 4 large eggs
- 1 tbsp black molasses
- 1 cup (3 oz/85g) blanched almonds, chopped
- 3/4 cup (3 oz/75g) self-rising flour
- 1½ cups (6 oz/175g) all-purpose flour
- 1½ level tsp pumpkin pie spice
- 1 lb (450g) almond paste (recipe follows)
- 3 tbsp apricot jam, warmed
- 1½ lb (675g) royal icing (recipe follows)

1 Put the fruit and cherries in a container, pour over the sherry and stir in the orange zest. Cover with a lid and leave to soak for at least 3 days, stirring daily.

2 Preheat the oven to 275°F/Confection 250°F. Grease a deep, 9 in round cake tin and line with nonstick baking paper.

3 Measure the butter, sugar, eggs, molasses and almonds into a very large bowl and beat well with a wooden spoon. Sift together the flours and spice and add to the bowl. Mix together until well blended. Stir in the soaked fruit and sherry.

4 Turn the mixture into the tin and level the top. Bake in the center of the preheated oven for 4–4½ hours, or until firm to the touch and a rich golden brown. Check after 2 hours and if the cake is the perfect color, cover with foil for the remainder of the cooking. A skewer inserted into the center of the cake should come out clean.

5 Cool completely in the tin.

6 Liberally dust a work surface with confectioners' sugar and roll out the marzipan to about 2 in larger than the surface of the cake. Brush the cake with apricot jam then carefully lift the almond paste over the cake. Gently level and smooth with the rolling pin, easing the almond paste down the sides of the cake.

7 Spread the icing evenly over the top and sides of the cake with an offset spatula. Leave the cake loosely covered overnight for the icing to harden a little.

ALMOND PASTE

To cover a 9 in round cake.

1¼ cups (5 oz/150g) confectioners' sugar
2½ cups (9 oz/250g) almond flour
½ cup plus 1 tbsp (5 oz/150g) superfine sugar
1 large egg
1 tsp almond extract

1 Sift the confectioners' sugar into a bowl, add the almond flour and sugar and mix well.

2 Add the egg and almond extract then work the mixture into a small smooth ball by hand—but do not over knead.

3 Cover with plastic wrap and store in the fridge until required.

ROYAL ICING

To cover a 9 in round cake.

3 large egg whites
1½ lb (675g) confectioners' sugar, sifted
3 tsp lemon juice
1½ tsp glycerin

1 Whisk the egg whites in a large bowl until they become frothy.

2 Add the confectioners' sugar, a spoonful at a time, then add the lemon juice and glycerin. Beat the icing until it is very stiff and white and will stand up in peaks.

3 Cover the surface of the icing tightly with plastic wrap and keep in a cool place until needed.

MAKING TIME 10 MINUTES
BAKING TIME 25 MINUTES

BANBURY TART

Although I live near Banbury, I have never managed to buy a Banbury cake there; I am told that they take too long to make. So I make it myself and it takes no time at all!

SERVES 8

2 tbsp (1 oz/30g) butter
1 tbsp (½ oz/15g) all-purpose flour
1 cup (5 oz/150g) currants
¼ cup (2 oz/50g) light muscovado sugar
a little grated nutmeg
2 tbsp sherry or rum
½ x 1.1 lb (490g) package puff pastry
a little milk, to glaze
confectioners' sugar, to dust

1 Preheat the oven to 425°F/Convection 375°F.

2 To make the filling, melt the butter in a saucepan over low heat and stir in the flour. Cook for 1 minute. Remove from the heat and add the currants, sugar, nutmeg and sherry or rum, mix well then leave to cool.

3 Meanwhile, cut the pastry in half. Roll out one piece and use it to line the base and sides of a 7 in square tin. Spread with the filling.

4 Roll out the remaining pastry, moisten the edges then cover the fruit with this pastry lid. Seal the edges firmly, brush the top with a little milk and make two cuts in the center of the pie.

5 Bake in the preheated oven for about 25 minutes, or until the pastry has risen and is golden brown.

6 Cool completely in the tin, then dust with confectioners' sugar before serving.

MAKING TIME 10–15 MINUTES
BAKING TIME 1 HOUR

DATE AND WALNUT CAKE

This is a cake with a lovely flavor. It is ideal to include in a packed lunch and it keeps very well.

MAKES 16 SQUARES

- ¾ cup (7 oz/200ml) boiling water
- 1 cup (6 oz/175g) semi-dried Medjool dates, stoned and chopped
- ¾ level tsp baking of soda
- 4 tbsp (2 oz/55g) butter, softened
- ½ cup plus 1 tbsp (6 oz/175g) light muscovado sugar
- 1 small egg, beaten
- 2 cups (8 oz/225g) all-purpose flour
- ¾ level tsp baking powder
- ½ cup (2 oz/50g) walnuts, chopped

1 Preheat the oven to 350°F/Convection 320°F. Grease an 8 in square cake tin and line with nonstick baking paper.

2 Measure the water, dates and baking soda into a bowl and leave to stand for 5 minutes.

3 Cream the butter and sugar together then beat in the egg, together with the water and date mixture.

4 Sift the flour with the baking powder and salt and fold into the fruit mixture, together with the walnuts.

5 Turn the mixture into the tin, level the top and bake in the preheated oven for about 1 hour. A skewer inserted into the center of the cake should come out clean.

6 Turn out, remove the paper and cool completely on a wire rack. Cut into 16 squares to serve.

BREAD

MAKING TIME 15 MINUTES
CHILLING TIME 4 HOURS

FRUIT AND NUT FRIDGE CAKE

This cake needs about 4 hours in the fridge to set, and it's rather rich—so only serve in thin slices!

MAKES 16 SLICES

- 12 tbsp (6 oz/170g) unsalted butter
- 4 heaped tbsp golden syrup (available online)
- 4 oz (100g) glacé cherries, chopped, rinsed and thoroughly dried
- ⅔ cup (4 oz/115g) dried dates, stoned and chopped
- ¾ cup (4 oz/100g) seedless raisins
- 1⅛ cups (4 oz/100g) walnuts, roughly chopped
- 8 oz (225g) graham crackers broken into large crumbs

1 Line an 8 in loose-bottomed cake or springform tin with nonstick baking paper.

2 Measure the butter and golden syrup into a heavy-bottomed pan and heat over low until the butter has melted. Increase the heat and boil for about 3 minutes, stirring all the time. Remove from the heat and set aside to cool.

3 Place all the remaining ingredients in a large bowl and pour over the cooled sauce. Mix well until evenly coated.

4 Turn the mixture into the tin and leave to chill in the fridge for about 4 hours, until set.

5 Turn out and cut into thin slices to serve.

CHAPTER FIVE

LITTLE CAKES, BUNS AND PASTRIES

MAKING TIME 10 MINUTES
BAKING TIME 20 MINUTES

SIMPLE QUEEN CAKES

From this basic mixture a variety of other small cakes can be made. You could add 2 tbsp currants for Currant Queen Cakes or 3 tbsp cocoa for Chocolate Queen Cakes. The number of liners required will vary slightly if the cakes are to be iced (see Iced Queen Cakes on page 164) or extra ingredients added. Make sure you stand the paper liners in a muffin tin as it helps to keep them in a good shape and prevents the cakes toppling over.

MAKES 12

- 10 tbsp (5 oz/140g) margarine, from fridge
- ½ cup plus 1 tbsp (5 oz/150g) superfine sugar
- 1¼ cups (5 oz/150g) self-rising flour
- 3 large eggs
- 1 level tsp baking powder

1 Preheat the oven to 400°F/Convection 350°F and arrange 12 paper liners in a muffin tin.

2 Measure all the ingredients into a large bowl and beat with an electric mixer until well blended and smooth.

3 Divide the mixture among the liners and bake in the preheated oven for about 20 minutes, or until the cakes are well risen and golden brown.

4 Lift out and cool on a wire rack.

MAKING TIME 10 MINUTES
BAKING TIME 15 MINUTES

ICED ORANGE QUEEN CAKES

Make sure that you do not fill the liners too full—leave about 1cm (½ in) between the mixture and the top of the liner before baking. You could also make these cakes using lemon zest and lemon juice instead.

MAKES 24

½ cup (4 oz/114g) margarine from fridge
½ cup (4 oz/100g) superfine sugar
1 cup (4 oz/100g) self-rising flour
2 large eggs
½ level tsp baking powder
finely grated zest of 1 small orange

For the icing

juice of 1 small orange
3¼ cups (13 oz/375g) confectioners' sugar

1 Preheat the oven to 400°F/Convection 350°F and arrange 24 paper liners in two muffin tins.

2 Measure all the cake ingredients into a large bowl and beat with an electric mixer until well blended and smooth.

3 Divide the mixture among the liners—do not overfill as you need a little of the rim of the liner above the level of the cakes when they are baked so that it is easy to ice the top. Bake in the preheated oven for about 15 minutes, or until the cakes are well risen and golden brown.

4 Lift out and cool on a wire rack.

5 Use the juice to make a little glacé icing with the confectioners' sugar. Add a little bit of water, if necessary, to give a smooth coating consistency. Spoon over the top of the cakes and decorate as desired.

MAKING TIME 10 MINUTES
BAKING TIME 15 MINUTES

ICED QUEEN CAKES

When you ice the cakes, the icing should cover the top and touch the edge of the liners. If you want to have a variety of colors, divide the icing into separate bowls once it has been made and then color each one as desired. Depending on the size of your liners, you will have between 18 and 24 cakes.

MAKES 18–24

½ cup (4 oz/114g) margarine from fridge
½ cup (4 oz/100g) superfine sugar
1 cup (4 oz/100g) self-rising flour
2 large eggs
½ level tsp baking powder

For the icing

3¼ cups (13 oz/375g) confectioners' sugar
decorations, as liked

1 Preheat the oven to 400°F/Convection 350°F and arrange 24 paper liners in two muffin tins.

2 Place all the cake ingredients into a large bowl and beat with an electric mixer until well blended and smooth.

3 Divide the mixture among the liners—leave about ½ in between the mixture and the top of the liners. It is important not overfill the liners as you need a little of the rim of the liner above the level of the cakes when they are baked so that it is easy to ice the top. Bake in the preheated oven for about 15 minutes, or until the cakes are well risen and golden brown.

4 Lift out and cool on a wire rack.

5 To make the icing, mix the confectioners' sugar with 3–4 tablespoons of water to give a smooth coating consistency. Spoon over the cakes and decorate as liked.

MAKING TIME 10 MINUTES
BAKING TIME 20 MINUTES

COFFEE BUNS

By adding coffee to the basic queen cake recipe, you have a lovely variation on the original.

MAKES 12

- 1½ level tsp instant coffee granules
- 3 large eggs
- 10 tbsp (5 oz/140g) margarine, from fridge
- ½ cup plus 1 tbsp (5 oz/150g) superfine sugar
- 1¼ cups (5 oz/150g) self-rising flour
- 1 level tsp baking powder

For the icing

- 4 tbsp (2 oz/55g) butter, softened
- 1¼ cups (5 oz/150g) confectioners' sugar, sifted
- 2 tsp coffee extract

1 Preheat the oven to 400°F/Convection 350°F and arrange 12 paper liners in a muffin tin.

2 Dissolve the coffee granules in the eggs and then measure all the cake ingredients into a large mixing bowl and beat with an electric mixer until well blended and smooth.

3 Divide the mixture between the liners and bake in the preheated oven for about 20 minutes, or until the cakes are well risen and golden brown.

4 Lift out and cool on a wire rack.

5 To make the icing, blend the butter with the confectioners' sugar and coffee extract. Spread a little icing on the top of each cake so that the top is completely covered.

MAKING TIME 10 MINUTES
BAKING TIME 15–20 MINUTES

MOLASSES SPICE BUNS

These are quick to make and bake and are best eaten warm, straight from the oven.

MAKES 12

4 tbsp (2 oz/50g) black molasses
4 tbsp (2 oz/55g) margarine, from fridge
1½ cups (6 oz/175g) self-rising flour
½ cup (2.6 oz/75g) sultanas
¾ cup (3 oz/75g) light muscovado sugar
1 level tsp ground cinnamon
½ level tsp baking powder
1 large egg

1 Preheat the oven to 400°F/Convection 350°F and arrange 12 paper liners in a muffin tin.

2 Measure the molasses and margarine into a small saucepan and heat over low until the spread has melted. Remove from the heat and set aside to cool slightly.

3 Measure all the remaining ingredients into a bowl, stir in the molasses mixture and mix thoroughly.

4 Divide the mixture among the liners and bake in the preheated oven for 15–20 minutes, or until the buns are well risen and cooked.

5 Leave to cool in the tins for a few minutes, then lift out and serve while they are still warm.

MAKING TIME 10 MINUTES
BAKING TIME 15 MINUTES

BUTTERFLY CAKES

These little cakes are a classic and are a lovely alternative to a standard queen cake. You could flavor them with orange or lemon zest, or make coffee butterfly cakes by adding coffee extract to the basic mixture. These will have a better domed shape if they are cooked in a shallow muffin-top tin, rather than a high-sided muffin tin.

MAKES 12

- ½ cup (4 oz/114g) margarine, from fridge
- ½ cup (4 oz/100g) superfine sugar
- 1 cup (4 oz/100g) self-rising flour
- 2 large eggs
- ½ level tsp baking powder

For the icing

- 6 tbsp (3 oz/85g) butter, softened
- 1¼ cups (5 oz/150g) confectioners' sugar, sifted, plus extra to dust

1 Preheat the oven to 400°F/Convection 350°F and arrange 12 paper liners in a muffin tin.

2 Measure all of the cake ingredients into a large bowl and beat with an electric mixer until well blended and smooth.

3 Divide the mixture among the liners and bake in the preheated oven for about 15 minutes, or until the cakes are well risen and golden brown.

4 Lift out and cool on a wire rack.

5 To make the icing, beat the butter and confectioners' sugar together until well blended and smooth.

6 Cut a slice from the top of each cake and cut this slice in half. Pipe a swirl of butter icing in the center of each cake and then replace the two half slices of cake into the icing, butterfly fashion. Dust with confectioners' sugar before serving.

MAKING TIME 10 MINUTES
BAKING TIME 15 MINUTES

LEMON AND CHERRY BUNS

These are the sort of small cakes that are ideal to give as a contribution for a coffee morning.

MAKES 12

4 tbsp (2 oz/55g) margarine, from fridge
¼ cup (2 oz/50g) superfine sugar
1 large egg, beaten
¾ cup (3 oz/75g) self-rising flour
1/4 cup (2 oz/50g) semolina
½ level tsp baking powder
finely grated zest of 1 lemon
3 tbsp milk

For the topping

¾ cup (3 oz/75g) confectioners' sugar, sifted
juice of about ½ lemon
6 glacé cherries, halved

1 Preheat the oven to 375°F/Convection 325°F and arrange 12 paper liners in a muffin tin.

2 Measure all the cake ingredients into a bowl and beat with an electric mixer until well blended.

3 Divide the mixture among the liners and bake in the preheated oven for about 15 minutes, or until risen and golden brown.

4 Lift out and cool on a wire rack.

5 To make the topping, mix the confectioners' sugar with sufficient lemon juice to give a spreading consistency. Spread a little on top of each bun and decorate with a cherry.

MAKING TIME 10 MINUTES
BAKING TIME 15 MINUTES

MOCHA BUNS

I always stand the paper liners in a muffin tin so that the buns keep a good round shape.

MAKES 12

1 cup (4 oz/100g) self-rising flour
½ level tsp baking powder
2 tbsp (1 oz/25g) semolina
5 tbsp (3 oz/75g) margarine, from fridge
¼ cup (2 oz/50g) superfine sugar
1 large egg, beaten
3 tbsp milk
1 tbsp coffee extract

For the icing

3 tbsp (1½ oz/42g) butter, softened
3 tbsp (1 oz/25g) cocoa powder, sifted
about 2 tbsp milk
1 cup (4 oz/100g) confectioners' sugar, sifted

1 Preheat the oven to 375°F/Convection 325°F and arrange 12 paper liners in a muffin tin.

2 Measure all the bun ingredients into a bowl and beat with an electric mixer until well blended and smooth.

3 Divide the mixture among the paper liners and bake in the preheated oven for about 15 minutes, or until well risen.

4 Lift out and cool on a wire rack.

5 To make the icing, measure all the ingredients into a bowl and beat well until smooth. Spread a little on top of each bun, then leave to set.

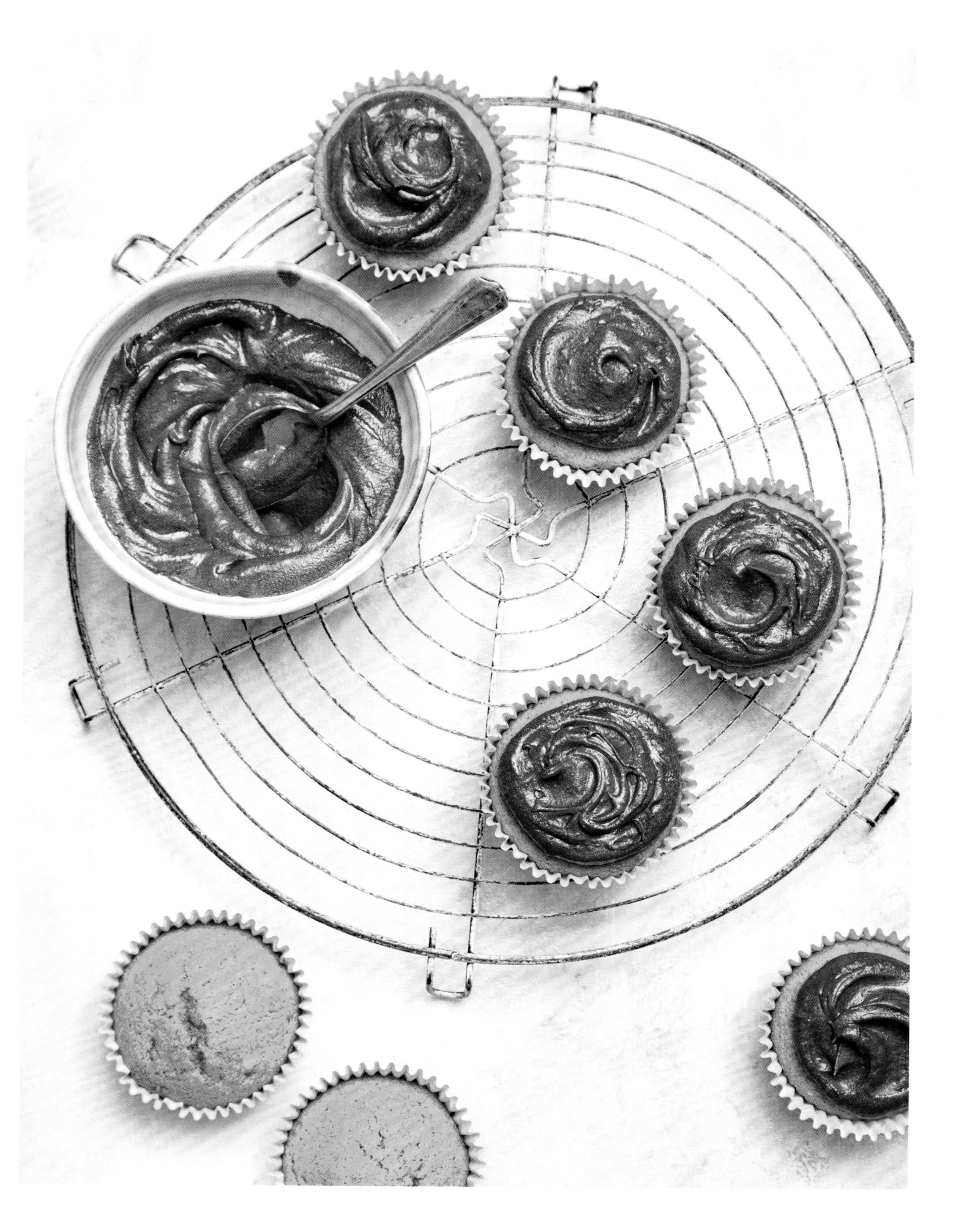

MAKING TIME 10 MINUTES
BAKING TIME 15–20 MINUTES

STICKY GINGER BUNS

These ginger buns—the candied ginger and golden syrup give them a lovely flavor—are best eaten on the day they are made.

MAKES 12

1 cup (4 oz/100g) self-rising flour
½ cup (4 oz/114g) margarine, from fridge
3/4 cup (3 oz/75g) superfine sugar
2 tbsp golden syrup (available online)
1 level tsp baking powder
2 level tsp ground ginger
2 large eggs

For the icing

2 cups (8 oz/225g) confectioners' sugar, sifted
1 tbsp water
about 2 tbsp ginger syrup from the jar
1 oz (25g) candied ginger, drained and finely chopped

1 Preheat the oven to 350°F/Convection 320°F and arrange 12 paper liners in a muffin tin.

2 Measure all the bun ingredients into a large bowl and beat with an electric mixer until thoroughly blended.

3 Divide the mixture among the liners and bake in the preheated oven for 15–20 minutes, or until golden brown.

4 Lift out and cool on a wire rack.

5 To make the icing, measure the confectioners' sugar into a bowl and work in the water and sufficient syrup to give a smooth glacé icing. Spread a little on the top of each bun and allow to set. Decorate with the chopped ginger pieces.

MAKING TIME 10 MINUTES
BAKING TIME 20–25 MINUTES

PINEAPPLE BUNS

These are best eaten on the day they are prepared, otherwise the pineapple on top of the buns will lose its shine.

MAKES 12

- 1 x 8 oz (227g) can pineapple slices
- 4 tbsp (2 oz/55g) margine, from fridge
- 2 large eggs
- ½ cup (4 oz/100g) superfine sugar
- 1¼ cups (6 oz/175g) self-rising flour
- ½ level tsp baking powder
- 1 tbsp milk

For the icing

- 1 cup (4 oz/100g) confectioners' sugar, sifted
- 2 tsp pineapple juice

1 Preheat the oven to 350°F/Convection 320°F and arrange 12 paper liners in a muffin tin.

2 Drain the can of pineapple, reserving the juice for the icing and one of the slices for decoration.

3 Finely chop the remaining pineapple, drain well on paper towels and then put in a bowl with the remaining bun ingredients. Beat well with an electric mixer until thoroughly blended.

4 Divide the mixture among the liners and bake in the preheated oven for 20–25 minutes, or until golden brown.

5 Lift out and cool on a wire rack.

6 To make the icing, measure the confectioners' sugar into a bowl and mix with sufficient pineapple juice to give a smooth spreading consistency (about 2 teaspoons). Spread a little icing onto each bun. Cut the reserved pineapple slice into 12 pieces and use to decorate the buns.

MAKING TIME 10 MINUTES
BAKING TIME 20 MINUTES

PEPPERMINT CREAM CAKES

Don't be overgenerous with the peppermint extract—3 drops are just enough to give the icing a delicate peppermint flavor.

MAKES 12

1 level tbsp cocoa powder
1 tbsp hot water
½ cup (4 oz/114g) margarine, from fridge
½ cup (4 oz/100g) superfine sugar
1 cup (4 oz/100g) self-rising flour
1 level tsp baking powder
2 large eggs

For the topping

2 cups (8 oz/225g) confectioners' sugar, sifted
about 2 tbsp cold water
2–3 drops peppermint extract
2–3 drops green food coloring
chocolate peppermints or chocolate mint balls, to decorate (optional)

1 Preheat the oven to 350°F/Convection 320°F and arrange 12 paper liners in a muffin tin.

2 Measure the cocoa and hot water into a large bowl and blend together until smooth. Add the remaining cake ingredients and beat well with an electric mixer until thoroughly blended.

3 Divide the mixture among the liners and bake in the preheated oven for about 20 minutes, or until well risen and the tops of the sponges spring back when lightly pressed with a finger.

4 Lift out and leave to cool on a wire rack.

5 To make the icing, measure the confectioners' sugar into a bowl and add sufficient water to give a smooth coating consistency. Stir in the peppermint extract and food coloring and mix well. Spread a little of the icing on top of each cake and decorate with either a whole or half chocolate peppermint or a few chocolate mint balls, if using.

MAKING TIME 15 MINUTES
CHILLING TIME 30 MINUTES
BAKING TIME 30 MINUTES

APPLE AND MINCEMEAT SLICES

I often make these at Christmastime, as they are less time consuming than making individual pies. They're best eaten on the day they are made.

MAKES 24

- 3 cups (12 oz/350g) all-purpose flour
- 12 tbsp (6 oz/170g) butter
- 2 level tbsp confectioners' sugar, plus extra to dust
- 2 large eggs

For the filling

- ¾ cup (3 oz/75g) demerara sugar
- 1 cup (8 oz/225g) mincemeat
- finely grated zest and juice of 1 lemon
- 1 level tsp ground mixed spice
- 2 large Granny Smith apples, peeled, cored and sliced

1 You will need a 13 x 9 in Swiss roll tin.

2 Measure the flour and butter into a food processor and whizz until breadcrumb stage. Add the confectioners' sugar and eggs and whizz until a dough is formed. Knead into a ball. Place just over a third of the pastry in the fridge and roll out the remaining pastry until thin. Use to line the tin, prick the base, then leave in the fridge to chill for 30 minutes.

3 Preheat the oven to 400°F/Convection 350°F and put a large baking sheet in the oven to get hot.

4 To make the filling, measure all the ingredients into a bowl and mix well.

5 Spread the filling over the top of the pastry in the tin. Grate the remaining chilled pastry over the top of the filling using a coarse grater and bake on the baking sheet in the preheated oven for about 30 minutes, until pale golden brown on top and underneath.

6 Dredge with a little confectioners' sugar, then leave to cool in the tin.

7 Cut into 24 fingers to serve.

MAKING TIME 10 MINUTES
BAKING TIME 30–35 MINUTES

HONEY AND MINCEMEAT FINGERS

These fingers are the perfect treat for people who think they don't like mincemeat — they'll never know it's there! The mincemeat filling gives them a lovely flavor. The baked mixture may also be cut into large pieces and served as dessert. If liked, the top may be covered with a little glacé icing.

MAKES 10

- 1 cup (4 oz/100g) self-rising flour
- ½ level tsp baking powder
- 6 tbsp (3 oz/85g) butter, softened
- ¼ cup (2 oz/50g) superfine sugar
- ¾ cup (3 oz/75g) quick oats
- 3 level tbsp honey
- 1 cup (8 oz/225g) mincemeat
- demerara sugar, to sprinkle

1 Preheat the oven to 350°F/Convection 320°F and grease a 7 in square tin with butter.

2 Place all the ingredients except for the mincemeat and demerara sugar into a bowl and mix well with a wooden spoon to form a soft dough. Divide the mixture in half. Put one half of the mixture into the tin and press with a spoon to cover the base.

3 Spread the mincemeat over the top, then dot with the remaining mixture. Gently spread the mixture out using a palette knife to completely cover the mincemeat. Sprinkle with demerara sugar.

4 Bake in the preheated oven for 30–35 minutes, or until golden brown.

5 Leave to cool in the tin for 20 minutes then mark into 10 fingers. Serve when completely cool.

MAKING TIME 15 MINUTES
BAKING TIME 3–4 HOURS

CLASSIC SIMPLE MERINGUES

Make meringues by this foolproof method and I guarantee success. Use nonstick silicone mats, which can be brushed off and used again and again. You can make these with light muscovado sugar, in which case they will be slightly darker when they are cooked than these very pale, off-white meringues.

MAKES 12 DOUBLE MERINGUES

- 4 large egg whites
- 1 cup (8 oz/225g) superfine sugar
- 1¼ cups (10 oz/300ml) heavy cream, whipped

1 Preheat the oven to 225°F/Convection 175°F and line two baking sheets with silicone mats.

2 Place the egg whites in a large bowl and beat on high speed with an electric hand-held mixer until they form soft peaks.

3 Add the sugar, a generous teaspoonful at a time, beating well after each addition, until all the sugar has been added.

4 Using two teaspoons, spoon the meringue out onto the baking sheets, putting 12 meringues on each tray.

5 Bake in the preheated oven for 3–4 hours, or until the meringues are firm and dry and will lift easily from the silicone mats. They will be a very pale off-white.

6 Whisk the cream until it is thick and use it to sandwich the meringues together.

MAKING TIME 10–15 MINUTES
BAKING TIME 15 MINUTES

JUST ROCK CAKES

Good old-fashioned rock cakes—quick and inexpensive to make. Eat on the day of baking as they are at their very best eaten fresh. They will freeze beautifully, too, so if you know that you are not going to eat them all in one sitting, freeze the remainder as soon as they are cool. If you like a spicier flavor, add ½ level teaspoon of mixed spice with the flour.

MAKES 12

- 2 cups (8 oz/225g) self-rising flour
- ½ cup (4 oz/114g) margarine, from fridge
- ¼ cup (2 oz/50g) granulated sugar
- 1½ cups (8 oz/225g) sultanas
- 1 large egg
- about 1 tbsp milk
- about 2 tbsp (1 oz/25g) demerara sugar

1 Preheat the oven to 400°F/Convection 350°F and grease two large baking sheets generously.

2 Measure the flour into a large bowl and rub in the margarine until the mixture resembles fine breadcrumbs. Add the sugar and fruit and toss together to mix. Add the egg and milk and blend to a really stiff mixture; if still too dry, add a little more milk.

3 Using two teaspoons, shape the mixture into 12 rough mounds on the baking sheets, sprinkle with the demerara sugar and bake in the preheated oven for about 15 minutes, until pale golden brown at the edges.

4 Lift off with an offset spatula and leave to cool on a wire rack.

MAKING TIME 20–25 MINUTES
BAKING TIME 35 MINUTES

COCONUT MERINGUE SLICES

These delicious fingers of sponge keep well. For a change, sprinkle the top with finely chopped glacé cherries.

MAKES 16

6 tbsp (3 oz/85g) margarine, from fridge
½ cup (4 oz/100g) superfine sugar
2 large egg yolks
2 tbsp milk
a few drops vanilla extract
1½ cups (6 oz/175g) self-rising flour

For the topping

2 large egg whites
½ cup (4 oz/100g) superfine sugar
½ cup (2 oz/50g) desiccated coconut
slivered almonds

1 Preheat the oven to 320°F/Convection 270°F and line an 11 x 7 in baking tin with nonstick baking paper.

2 Cream the margarine and sugar together until soft. Beat in the egg yolks, milk and vanilla extract and lastly fold in the flour—the mixture will be quite stiff. Spread it carefully in a smooth layer over the base of the tin.

3 Place the egg whites in a large bowl and whisk with an electric whisk until stiff. Add in the sugar a generous teaspoonful at a time. Fold in the desiccated coconut. Spread over the cake mixture and sprinkle with the slivered almonds.

4 Bake in the preheated oven for about 35 minutes, by which time the meringue will be firm to the touch and a pale golden brown.

5 Cool completely in the tin.

6 Cut into 16 slices to serve.

MAKING TIME 5 MINUTES
BAKING TIME 20–25 MINUTES

CHEWY DATE BARS

These are so good—ideal to pop into a lunch box. Store them in an airtight container.

MAKES 16

½ cup (4 oz/114g) margarine, from fridge
½ cup (4 oz/100g) granulated sugar
2 large eggs
1 cup (4 oz/100g) all-purpose flour
1 tsp vanilla extract
⅔ cup (4 oz/115g) semi-dried Medjool dates, pitted and finely chopped

1 Preheat the oven to 350°F/Convection 320°F. Grease and flour a 7 in square tin.

2 Measure all the ingredients, except the dates, into a large bowl and beat with an electric mixer until well blended and smooth. Stir in the dates.

3 Turn the mixture into the tin and smooth flat. Bake in the preheated oven for 20–25 minutes, until a pale golden brown all over.

4 Cool completely in the tin.

5 Cut into 16 bars to serve.

MAKING TIME 20 MINUTES
BAKING TIME 40 MINUTES

ORANGE FRUIT CRUNCH FINGERS

These are lovely in a lunch box or served warm, as dessert, with ice cream.

MAKES 8

finely grated zest and juice of 1 orange
⅓ cup (2 oz/60g) semi-dried Medjool dates, pitted and chopped or cut with scissors
¼ cup (1.3 oz/40g) seedless raisins
1 cup (3½ oz/100g) quick oats
⅓ (1½ oz/40g) all-purpose flour
⅓ cup (1½ oz/40g) demerara sugar
6 tbsp (3 oz/85g) butter

1 Preheat the oven to 375°F/Convection 325°F and grease 7 in square tin.

2 Combine the orange juice to ½ cup (4 oz/120ml) with water and put in a small saucepan. Add the dates and raisins and cook over low heat until the mixture is thick—this will take about 10 minutes. Turn out onto a flat plate, spread out and leave to cool.

3 Meanwhile, measure the oats, flour and sugar into a large bowl with the zest and rub in the butter. Press half this mixture into the tin and cover with the cooled fruit. Sprinkle with the remaining mixture, press down lightly and bake in the preheated oven for about 40 minutes.

4 Leave to cool in the tin for 20 minutes, then mark into 8 fingers and leave to cool completely.

MAKING TIME 10 MINUTES
BAKING TIME 25–30 MINUTES

BLUEBERRY MUFFINS

These are quick, easy and perfect for breakfast or the lunch box.

MAKES 12

2 large eggs
¾ cup (3 oz/75g) superfine sugar
1 cup (8 oz/225ml) milk
½ cup (4 oz/114g) butter, melted and cooled
1 tsp vanilla extract
finely grated zest of 1 lemon
2½ cups (10 oz/275g) self-rising flour
1 level tsp baking powder
7 oz (200g) blueberries

1 Preheat the oven to 400°F/Convection 350°F and arrange 12 paper liners in a muffin tin.

2 Measure the eggs, sugar, milk, butter, vanilla and lemon zest into a large bowl and beat with an electric mixer. Sift in the flour and baking powder and beat again until just blended.

3 Finally, fold in the blueberries then spoon into the liners. Bake in the preheated oven for 25–30 minutes, until well risen and lightly golden brown.

4 Lift out and cool on a wire rack.

MAKING TIME 20 MINUTES
BAKING TIME 35 MINUTES

MARMALADE SURPRISE CAKES

If desired these small cakes can be iced with a little orange glacé icing.

MAKES 24

2 cups (8 oz/225g) all-purpose flour
½ cup (4 oz/114g) butter
about 8 tsp water
about 4 tbsp orange marmalade
confectioners' sugar, to dust

For the topping

½ cup (4 oz/114g) margarine, from fridge
½ cup (4 oz/100g) superfine sugar
2 large eggs
1 cup (4 oz/100g) self-rising flour
½ level tsp baking powder
finely grated zest of 1 orange

1 Preheat the oven to 350°F/Convection 320°F. You will need two 12-hole muffin tins.

2 Measure the flour into a bowl and rub in the butter until the mixture resembles fine breadcrumbs. Mix to a firm dough with the water. Knead until smooth then roll out on a lightly floured surface. Cut out 24 circles with a 3 in fluted pastry cutter and use to line the muffin tins.

3 Place ½ teaspoonful of marmalade in each pastry case.

4 To make the topping, measure all the ingredients into a mixing bowl and beat with an electric mixer until well blended.

5 Spoon teaspoonfuls of the mixture on top of the marmalade to completely cover then bake in the preheated oven for about 35 minutes, until the topping is golden brown and the pastry is cooked underneath.

6 Leave to cool in the tins for a few moments then lift out carefully with a knife and finish cooling on a wire rack. Dust with confectioners' sugar to serve.

MAKING TIME 10 MINUTES
CHILLING TIME 30 MINUTES
BAKING TIME 15 MINUTES

STRAWBERRY CREAM TARTS

If you have a glut of raspberries use them in place of strawberries. These little tarts are delicious to eat, sitting outside, at a special summer coffee party.

MAKES 6

1 (15 oz) ready-to-bake pie crust
¾ cup (6 oz/180ml) heavy cream
1 level tbsp confectioners' sugar
½ tsp vanilla extract
12 oz (350g) strawberries, hulled and each cut into 3 slices
3 tbsp redcurrant jelly

1 You will need six 3 in loose-bottomed fluted mini tart tins.

2 Unroll the pastry onto a lightly floured surface and roll to a slightly thinner thickness. Stamp out 6 circles with a 5 in round cutter and use to line the tins. Prick the bases and sides with a fork and leave to chill for about 30 minutes.

3 Preheat the oven to 400°F/Convection 350°F.

4 Line each tart with a small piece of baking paper, weigh down with pie weights and bake in the preheated oven for 10 minutes.

5 Remove the paper and weights and bake for 5 minutes more, until pale golden and crisp.

6 Remove from the oven and leave to cool on a wire rack.

7 Meanwhile, whisk the cream with the confectioners' sugar and vanilla to soft peaks. Divide among the cooled pastry cases and arrange the strawberries on top.

8 Melt the redcurrant jelly with 1 tablespoon of water in a small pan over low heat, stirring until smooth, and then spoon or brush over the tarts. Leave to set.

MAKING TIME 20 MINUTES
BAKING TIME 20–25 MINUTES

YORKSHIRE CAKES

These are delicious small tarts with a spongy filling.

MAKES 24
2 cups (8 oz/225g) all-purpose flour
½ cup (4 oz/114g) butter
about 8 tsp water
about 4 tbsp raspberry jam

For the topping
½ cup (4 oz/114g) margarine, from fridge
1 cup (8 oz/225g) superfine sugar
2 large eggs
½ cup (3½ oz/100g) semolina or ground rice
⅓ cup (1.8 oz/50g) currants

1 Preheat the oven to 400°F/Convection 350°F. You will need two 12-hole muffin tins.

2 Measure the flour into a bowl and rub in the butter until the mixture resembles fine breadcrumbs. Mix to a firm dough with the water. Knead until smooth, then roll out on a lightly floured surface. Cut out 24 circles with a 3 in cutter and use to line the muffin tins.

3 Spoon ½ teaspoon of jam into the bottom of each pastry case.

4 To make the topping, measure all the ingredients into a bowl and beat with an electric mixer until well blended.

5 Spoon teaspoonfuls of the mixture on top of the jam to cover, then bake in the preheated oven for 20–25 minutes, until the topping is golden brown and the pastry is cooked underneath.

6 Leave to cool in the tins for a few moments then lift out carefully with a knife and finish cooling on a wire rack.

MAKING TIME 10 MINUTES
BAKING TIME 30 MINUTES

QUICK BAKLAVA

Serve this pastry warm with whipped cream. Filo pastry is readily available from good Greek shops, delicatessens and most supermarkets.

MAKES 16

9 oz (250g) filo pastry
½ cup (4 oz/114g) unsalted butter, melted
grated zest and juice of 1 lemon
1 cup (3½ oz/100g) walnuts, finely chopped
2 tbsp (1 oz/25g) demerara sugar

For the syrup

½ cup (4 oz/120ml) water
1 cup (8 oz/225g) superfine sugar

1 Preheat the oven to 400°F/Convection 350°F and lightly butter an 11 x 7 in baking tin.

2 Cut the pastry sheets in half so that they are roughly the size of the tin. Lay 1 sheet of pastry in the tin, brush with melted butter and continue until there are 8 layers of pastry in the tin. Brush the top layer with melted butter and sprinkle with the lemon zest, nuts and sugar. Continue to add 8 more layers of pastry, brushing with butter between each layer. Finally, brush the top with more butter then cut the pastry with a very sharp knife into 16 equal-sized pieces.

3 Bake in the preheated oven for about 30 minutes, until pale golden brown.

4 Leave to cool in the tin.

5 To make the syrup, measure the water and sugar into a pan and slowly bring it to the boil. Simmer for about 15 minutes without a lid to give a light syrup.

6 Remove from the heat, stir in the lemon juice, and pour over the baklava.

MAKING TIME 15 MINUTES
CHILLING TIME 30 MINUTES
BAKING TIME 16 MINUTES

PALMIERS

Best eaten when freshly made. These are good served with ice cream.

MAKES 24

- 1 (1.1 lb/490g) puff pastry all-purpose flour
- ½ cup (4 oz/100g) demerara sugar
- 1 level tsp ground cinnamon
- a little milk, to glaze
- 1 large egg white, beaten with a fork

1 Unroll the pastry and dust lightly with flour. Place nonstick baking paper over the top of the pastry and roll out to a slightly thinner rectangle measuring 13 x 11 in. Sprinkle one half of the pastry with half the demerara sugar and all of the cinnamon. Fold the pastry in half to cover the sugar. Reroll the pastry to a rectangle measuring 11 x 9 in. Brush the surface with a little milk, then carefully roll both short sides into the center of the pastry to make two tight rolls. Leave to chill in the fridge for 30 minutes.

2 Preheat the oven to 425°F/Convection 375°F and line two large baking sheets with nonstick baking paper.

3 Slice the pastry into ½-in slices to make 24 palmiers and place on the baking sheets. Brush with a little beaten egg white and sprinkle with half the remaining sugar. Bake in the preheated oven for 8 minutes.

4 Remove the palmiers from the oven, turn them over and brush the tops with more beaten egg white. Sprinkle with the remaining demerara and return them to the oven for 8 minutes more, until golden brown on both sides.

5 Lift off with a spatula and leave to cool on a wire rack.

CHAPTER SIX

BISCUITS AND COOKIES

MAKING TIME 10 MINUTES
BAKING TIME 55 MINUTES

PROPER SHORTBREAD

Delicious with a cup of tea.

MAKES 24

- 1 cup (8 oz/225g) butter, softened
- ½ cup (4 oz/100g) superfine sugar
- 2 cups (8 oz/225g) all-purpose flour
- ½ cup (4 oz/100g) semolina
- 2 level tbsp demerara sugar

1 Preheat the oven to 320°F/Convection 270°F. You will need a 12 x 9 in traybake tin.

2 Cream the butter and sugar together in a mixing bowl. Work in the flour and semolina and bring together using your hands into a soft dough.

3 Press the mixture into the tin, level and smooth the top using the back of a spoon, and sprinkle with demerara sugar. Bake in the preheated oven for about 55 minutes, until a pale golden brown.

4 Remove from the oven, leave for 5 minutes, then mark into 24 triangles. Leave in the tin to cool completely before lifting out onto a wire rack.

MAKING TIME 10 MINUTES
BAKING TIME 50–55 MINUTES

LEMON SHORTBREAD

This really is quite one of my favorite shortbreads. It keeps extremely well in an airtight container and is delicious to serve with a cup of coffee.

MAKES 12

½ cup (4 oz/114g) butter, softened
¼ cup (2 oz/50g) superfine sugar, plus extra to sprinkle
1 cup (4 oz/100g) all-purpose flour
scant ½ cup (2 oz/50g) corn starch
finely grated zest of 1 large lemon

1 Preheat the oven to 320°F/Convection 270°F. You will need a 7 in square tin.

2 Cream the butter and sugar together in a bowl until light and fluffy. Work in the flour, corn starch and lemon zest and knead well together.

3 Press the mixture into the tin, level and smooth the top using the back of a spoon. Bake in the preheated oven for 50–55 minutes, until a pale golden brown.

4 Remove from the oven and mark into 12 fingers. Cool completely in the tin, then lift out onto a wire rack.

5 Sprinkle with sugar to serve.

MAKING TIME 10 MINUTES
BAKING TIME 50–55 MINUTES

APRICOT SHORTBREAD

Apricots are added to this basic shortbread to give it a nice flavor and texture. This is a good recipe to prepare for a bazaar or for a bake sale.

MAKES 12

- ½ cup (4 oz/114g) butter, softened
- ¼ cup (2 oz/50g) superfine sugar
- 1 cup (4 oz/100g) all-purpose flour
- scant ½ cup (2 oz/50g) corn starch
- ¼ cup (1.3 oz/40g) ready-to-eat dried apricots, finely chopped
- confectioners' sugar, sifted

1 Preheat the oven to 320°F/Convection 270°F. You will need a 7 in square tin.

2 Cream the butter and sugar together in a bowl until light and fluffy. Work in the flour, corn starch and the apricots and knead well together.

3 Press the mixture into the tin, level and smooth the top using the back of a spoon. Bake in the preheated oven for 50–55 minutes, until a very pale golden brown.

4 Remove from the oven and mark into 12 fingers. Cool completely in the tin, then lift out onto a wire rack.

5 Sprinkle with confectioners' sugar to serve.

MAKING TIME 15 MINUTES
BAKING TIME 40 MINUTES

VIENNESE FINGER BISCUITS

This is a basic recipe that can be adapted very easily to make all sorts of interesting biscuits.

MAKES 25–30

1 cup (8 oz/225g) butter, softened
½ cup (2 oz/50g) confectioners' sugar
2 cups (8 oz/225g) all-purpose flour
1 tsp vanilla extract

1 Preheat the oven to 325°F/Convection 270°F and line two baking sheets with nonstick baking paper.

2 Put the ingredients into a food processor and whizz until you have a smooth, soft dough.

3 Place the mixture in a piping bag fitted with a large star nozzle and pipe out into 2–3 in lengths. If time allows, leave to chill in the fridge for 30 minutes, until very firm.

4 Bake the biscuits in the preheated oven for about 40 minutes, until light, pale golden brown at the edges.

5 Leave to cool on the sheets for a few moments, then lift off with a an offset spatula and finish cooling on a wire rack.

VARIATION: CHOCOLATE FINGERS

Make and pipe as in the basic recipe. When completely cool, dip the ends of the biscuits in a little melted chocolate and leave to set on a wire rack.

MAKING TIME 15 MINUTES
CHILLING TIME 30 MINUTES
BAKING TIME 10 MINUTES

TRADITIONAL DUTCH BUTTER BISCUITS

These biscuits really should be made with butter as the flavor of margarine doesn't do them justice.

MAKES ABOUT 20

- 1 cup (8 oz/225g) unsalted butter, softened
- ½ cup (4 oz/100g) superfine sugar
- 1 large egg yolk
- 1¾ cups (7 oz/200g) all-purpose flour
- ¾ cups (3 oz/75g) almond flour
- a little confectioners, sugar, to dust

1 Line two or three large baking sheets with nonstick baking paper.

2 Measure all the ingredients except the confectioners' sugar into a large mixing bowl and work together until thoroughly mixed and smooth (this can be done most quickly in a food processor or mixer).

3 Place the mixture in a piping bag fitted with a large rose nozzle and pipe the mixture into rounds on the prepared baking sheets. Leave to chill in the fridge for 30 minutes, until firm.

4 Preheat the oven to 375°F/Convection 325°F.

5 Bake in the preheated oven for about 10 minutes, until just beginning to color at the edges.

6 Leave to cool on the sheets for a few moments, then lift off with an offset spatula and finish cooling on a wire rack.

7 Serve dusted with a little confectioners' sugar.

MAKING TIME 15 MINUTES
BAKING TIME 12 MINUTES

CINNAMON CRISPY BISCUITS

Lovely crunchy biscuits, always popular in our cookie jar.

MAKES ABOUT 36

1 cup (8 oz/225g) butter, softened
1 cup (8 oz/225g) demerara sugar
2 cups (8 oz/225g) self-rising flour
½ level tsp pumpkin pie spice
2 level tsp ground cinnamon
1 large egg, beaten

1 Heat the oven to 400°F/Convection 350°F and line three large baking sheets with nonstick baking paper, or bake in batches.

2 Measure all the ingredients into a mixing bowl and beat with an electric mixer until well blended and smooth.

3 Roll the mixture into small balls and place onto the baking sheets. Press down slightly to flatten the balls and bake in the preheated oven for about 12 minutes, until golden brown.

4 Leave to cool on the sheets for a few moments, then lift off with an offset spatula and finish cooling on a wire rack.

MAKING TIME 15 MINUTES
BAKING TIME 12 MINUTES

DANISH LACE BISCUITS

These are very thin almondy biscuits, which are good to serve with cold desserts.

MAKES ABOUT 24

½ cup (2 oz/50g) blanched almonds, chopped
¾ cup (3 oz/75g) all-purpose flour
⅔ cup (3 oz/75g) superfine sugar
6 tbsp (3 oz/85g) butter, softened

1 Preheat the oven to 350°F/Convection 320°F and line four large baking sheets with nonstick baking paper, or bake in batches using two large baking sheets.

2 Measure all the ingredients into a bowl and work together with a wooden spoon to form a firm dough. Knead gently until smooth.

3 Take teaspoonfuls of the mixture, roll into balls and arrange on the baking sheets, leaving plenty of room for them to spread. Press down with a fork to flatten them, then reshape to a circle with the back of the fork.

4 Bake in the preheated oven for about 12 minutes, until just beginning to turn golden brown at the edges.

5 Leave to cool on the sheets for a moment, then lift off with on offset spatula on to a wire rack to finish cooling.

MAKING TIME 5 MINUTES
BAKING TIME 8–10 MINUTES

ALMOND CRISPS

These biscuits are perfect to serve with mousses and fools. They seem to lose their flavor quite quickly in a container so they are best served fresh.

MAKES ABOUT 18

5 tbsp (2½ oz/70g) butter, softened
¼ cup (2 oz/50g) superfine sugar
⅓ cup (1½ oz/40g) all-purpose flour
⅓ cup (1½ oz/40g) slivered almonds

1 Preheat the oven to 350°F/Convection 320°F and line a baking sheet with nonstick baking paper. You will need a couple of lightly oiled rolling pins.

2 Cream the butter and sugar until very pale then stir in the flour and almonds. Shape the mixture into marble-sized balls and place them about 3 in apart on the baking sheet. Only bake one sheet at a time (you will need to work fast once they are baked).

3 Flatten the balls with a damp fork and bake in the preheated oven for 8–10 minutes, until a pale golden brown.

4 Remove the biscuits from the oven, leave to cool for 30–60 seconds, then lift off each one very carefully with an offset spatula and lay over a lightly oiled rolling pin and leave to harden. They are very fragile so be light fingered!

5 When they have hardened, lift off very carefully and store in an airtight container.

MAKING TIME 10 MINUTES
BAKING TIME 15–20 MINUTES

OLD ENGLISH JUMBLES

Jumbles are traditionally made in the shape of an S. However, if time is short, you may find it quicker to roll the mixture out into small balls. Press them flat with two fingers before baking. These biscuits keep well if stored in an airtight container.

MAKES ABOUT 20

- 5 tbsp (2½ oz/70g) butter, softened
- ⅓ cup (2½ oz/65g) superfine sugar
- 1 large egg yolk
- finely grated zest of 1 lemon
- scant ¼ cup (1 oz/25g) almond flour
- 1¼ cups (5 oz/150g) all-purpose flour
- ½ level tsp pumpkin pie spice
- 1 tbsp milk

1 Preheat the oven to 350°F/Convection 320°F and line two baking sheets with nonstick baking paper.

2 Cream the butter with the sugar until light and fluffy. Beat in the egg yolk and all the remaining ingredients. If the dough is too stiff and crumbly to roll, add another tablespoon of milk.

3 Take small pieces of the dough, roll each out into a strip and then form into an S and lay it on the baking sheet. Repeat with the remaining dough. Bake in the preheated oven for 15–20 minutes, until tinged a pale golden brown at the edges.

4 Lift off with an offset spatula and cool completely on a wire rack.

MAKING TIME 20 MINUTES
BAKING TIME 15–20 MINUTES

HURDON FARMHOUSE BISCUITS

These biscuits are a bit fiddly to prepare, but it's worth persevering as the end result looks good and tastes delicious.

MAKES ABOUT 50

- 3 cups (12 oz/350g) self-rising flour
- 1 cup (8 oz/225g) butter
- ¾ cup (6 oz/175g) superfine sugar
- 1 large egg, beaten
- ¼ cup (1 oz/25g) rolled oats, to coat

1 Preheat the oven to 350°F/Convection 320°F and line two or three large baking sheets with nonstick baking paper, or bake in batches.

2 Measure the flour into a large bowl and rub in the butter until the mixture resembles fine breadcrumbs. Stir in the sugar and bind to a dough with the beaten egg. Knead until smooth.

3 Take teaspoonfuls of the mixture and roll them into balls. Press the balls down into the oats to flatten them into rounds and coat lightly with the oats. Arrange on the baking sheets and bake in the preheated oven for 15–20 minutes, until pale golden brown.

4 Leave to cool on the sheets for a few moments, then lift off with an offset spatula and finish cooling on a wire rack.

MAKING TIME 15 MINUTES
BAKING TIME 15–20 MINUTES

MUESLI JACKS

These biscuits are a good way of turning unwanted breakfast cereal into a family favorite. You can use any cereal, but we like adding one with fruit and nuts. If the cereal is particularly sweet, you could reduce the amount of demerara sugar.

MAKES ABOUT 24

- ½ cup (4 oz/114g) butter
- 1 rounded tbsp golden syrup
- ½ cup (4 oz/100g) demerara sugar
- ½ cup (3 oz/75g) mixed cereal with fruit and nuts
- ¾ cup (3 oz/75g) self-rising flour

1 Preheat the oven to 320°F/Convection 270°F and line three large baking sheets with nonstick baking paper, or bake in batches.

2 Measure the butter, syrup and sugar into a saucepan and place over a gentle heat until the butter has melted.

3 Remove from the heat and measure in the mixed cereal and flour. Stir well.

4 Allow the mixture to cool slightly, then roll into small balls and place them, well spaced, on the baking sheets. Bake in the preheated oven for 15–20 minutes, until a pale golden brown all over.

5 Leave to cool on the sheets for a few moments, then lift off with an offset spatula and finish cooling on a wire rack.

6 Store in an airtight container.

MAKING TIME 10 MINUTES
BAKING TIME 15 MINUTES

CHERRY AND NUT CRISPS

These small flapjack-type biscuits keep very well and have an excellent flavor.

MAKES ABOUT 30

½ cup (4 oz/100g) demerara sugar
½ cup (4 oz/114g) butter
⅓ cup (4 oz/90g) golden syrup (available online)
1 cup (4 oz/100g) all-purpose flour
¾ cup (3 oz/75g) rolled oats
¼ cup (1 oz/25g) almond flour
⅓ cup (1½ oz/40g) blanched almonds, chopped
2 oz (50g) glacé cherries, chopped

1 Preheat the oven to 350°F/Convection 320°F and line two or three large baking sheets with nonstick baking paper, or bake in batches.

2 Measure the sugar, butter and syrup into a saucepan and heat gently until the sugar has dissolved.

3 Remove from the heat, add all the remaining ingredients and mix very thoroughly. Leave to cool.

4 Roll the mixture into small balls, each about the size of a walnut, and place on the baking sheets. Flatten down slightly, allowing room for them to spread slightly and bake in the preheated oven for about 15 minutes, until a pale golden brown.

5 Leave to cool on the sheets for a few moments, then lift off with an offset spatula and finish cooling on a wire rack.

6 Store in an airtight container.

MAKING TIME 15 MINUTES
BAKING TIME 20 MINUTES

ABBEY BISCUITS

Delicious—always a favorite oaty biscuit with a cup of coffee.

MAKES ABOUT 40

- 1¼ cups (5 oz/150g) all-purpose flour
- 10 tbsp (5 oz/140g) butter, softened
- 1/2 cup plus 1 tbsp (5 oz/150g) superfine sugar
- 1 cup (4 oz/100g) rolled oats
- 1 tbsp milk
- 1 rounded tbsp golden syrup (available online)
- 1 level tsp baking soda

1 Preheat the oven to 320°F/Convection 270°F and line four large baking sheets with nonstick baking paper, or bake in batches.

2 Measure all the ingredients into a bowl and work together until thoroughly blended.

3 Take teaspoonfuls of the mixture, roll into balls and arrange on the prepared baking sheets, leaving room for them to spread. Bake in the preheated oven for about 20 minutes, until golden brown.

4 Leave to cool on the sheets for a few moments, then lift off with an offset spatula and finish cooling on a wire rack.

MAKING TIME 10 MINUTES
BAKING TIME 15 MINUTES

FAIRINGS

A crisp biscuit with a mild ginger flavor.

MAKES 24

1¼ cups (6 oz/175g) self-rising flour
1½ level tsp ground ginger
pinch of baking soda
⅔ cup (3 oz/75g) superfine sugar
6 tbsp (3 oz/85g) butter
1 tbsp golden syrup (available online)

1 Preheat the oven to 350°F/Convection 320°F and line three large baking sheets with nonstick baking paper, or bake in batches.

2 Sift the flour, ginger and baking soda together into a bowl.

3 Measure the sugar, butter and syrup into a saucepan and heat gently until the butter has melted.

4 Stir the melted mixture into the dry ingredients and mix to a stiff dough.

5 Shape into 24 small balls or place in teaspoonfuls on the baking sheets and bake in the preheated oven for about 15 minutes, until golden brown at the edges.

6 Leave to cool slightly, then lift off with an offset spatula and finish cooling on a wire rack.

MAKING TIME 15 MINUTES
BAKING TIME 10–15 MINUTES

SPICED BISCUIT THINS

A special ginger biscuit that is good to serve with ice creams and sorbets.

MAKES 28

- 1/3 cup (4 oz/115g) golden syrup (available online)
- 4 tbsp (2 oz/55g) butter
- 2 tbsp (1 oz/25g) demerara sugar
- 1 cup (4 oz/100g) all-purpose flour
- ½ level tsp baking soda
- 1½ level tsp ground ginger
- ½ level tsp pumpkin pie spice

1 Preheat the oven to 350°F/Convection 320°F and line two large baking sheets with nonstick baking paper.

2 Measure the syrup, butter and sugar into a pan and place over low heat until the butter has melted.

3 Measure the remaining ingredients into a bowl, add the melted mixture and beat well until thoroughly blended. Set aside to cool to room temperature.

4 Spoon teaspoonfuls of the mixture onto the baking sheets, leaving room for them to spread. Bake in the preheated oven for 10–15 minutes, until dark golden brown.

5 Leave to cool slightly, then lift off with an offset spatula and finish cooling on a wire rack.

MAKING TIME 15 MINUTES
CHILLING TIME 30 MINUTES
BAKING TIME 15 MINUTES

GINGER COOKIES

These can easily fit in with the rest of your plans for the day. The mixture can be prepared and left to chill while you are out shopping, then baked when you get back.

MAKES 36–40

- 12 tbsp (6 oz/170g) butter
- ½ cup (4½ oz/125g) light muscovado sugar
- 2 level tsp ground ginger
- 2 cups (8 oz/225g) all-purpose flour
- demerara sugar, to coat

1 Measure the butter and sugar into a bowl. Beat with an electric hand-held mixer until light and fluffy. Add the ginger and flour and beat into a soft dough.

2 Turn the dough out on to a lightly floured surface and knead until smooth. Roll into two sausage shapes about 7 in long and 2 in wide. Place each one on a sheet of plastic wrap and sprinkle generously with demerara sugar. Roll each sausage in the sugar until the surface is completely coated and the sugar is stuck to the dough. Wrap in the plastic wrap and leave to chill in the fridge for about 30 minutes, until very firm.

3 Preheat the oven to 350°F/Convection 320°F and line two large baking sheets with nonstick baking paper.

4 Cut each roll into 18–20 slices and arrange, well-spaced, on the prepared baking sheets. Bake in the preheated oven for about 15 minutes, until pale golden brown at the edges.

5 Leave to cool on the sheets for a few moments, then lift off with an offset spatula and finish cooling on a wire rack.

MAKING TIME 10 MINUTES
CHILLING TIME 30 MINUTES
BAKING TIME 15 MINUTES

GINGER AND CHOCOLATE CHIP SNAPS

These ginger biscuits are quick to make as there is no stamping out of rounds—just cutting slices from the roll.

MAKES 24

- 2 cups (8 oz/225g) all-purpose flour
- 1 level tsp ground ginger
- ¼ level tsp baking soda
- 5 tbsp (2½ oz/70g) butter
- ¼ cup (3 oz/90g) golden syrup (available online)
- ½ cup (4 oz/100g) semisweet chocolate chips

1 Sift the flour, ginger and baking soda into a bowl and rub in the butter until the mixture resembles breadcrumbs. Add the golden syrup and chocolate chips and mix into a stiff dough—it is easier to use your hands.

2 Roll the dough into a sausage about 9½ in in length, cover in plastic wrap and leave to chill in the fridge for about 30 minutes, until firm.

3 Preheat the oven to 400°F/Convection 350°F and line two large baking sheets with nonstick baking paper.

4 Cut the roll into about 24 thin slices and arrange on the baking sheets. Bake in the preheated oven for about 15 minutes, until a pale ginger color.

5 Lift off with an offset spatula and cool completely on a wire rack.

MAKING TIME 10 MINUTES
CHILLING TIME 30 MINUTES
BAKING TIME 25 MINUTES

BOTERMOPPEN

These are Dutch shortbread biscuits and have a lovely flavor.

MAKES 32

- 12 tbsp (6 oz/175g) unsalted butter
- finely grated zest of ½ lemon
- ½ cup (4 oz/100g) superfine sugar
- 2 cups (8 oz/225g) all-purpose flour
- 2 tbsp (1 oz/25g) granulated sugar

1 Cream the butter and lemon zest in a large bowl until soft, then beat in the sugar until the mixture is light. Blend in the flour and knead lightly until smooth (use your hands for this).

2 Divide the mixture in two and roll out to form two 6 in sausages. Coat these in granulated sugar, cover in plastic wrap and leave to chill in the fridge for about 30 minutes, until firm.

3 Preheat the oven to 320°F/Convection 270°F and line two or three large baking sheets with nonstick baking paper, or bake in batches.

4 Cut each sausage into 16 slices and place on the baking sheets, allowing a little room for them to spread. Bake in the preheated oven for about 25 minutes, until pale golden brown at the edges.

5 Remove from the oven and carefully lift off with an offset spatula to cool on a wire rack.

MAKING TIME 15 MINUTES
BAKING TIME 10–12 MINUTES

SULTANA WALNUT COOKIES

The sultanas and walnuts in these cookies combine well to give a very good flavor.

MAKES ABOUT 36

½ cup (4 oz/114g) butter, softened
½ cup (4 oz/100g) light muscovado sugar
1 large egg, beaten
½ level tsp baking soda
2 cups (8 oz/225g) all-purpose flour
3/4 cup (4 oz/100g) sultanas
1/2 cup (2 oz/50g) walnuts, chopped
finely grated zest of 1 orange

1 Preheat the oven to 350°F/Convection 320°F and line two baking sheets with nonstick baking paper.

2 Measure the butter and sugar into a bowl and beat well until soft and creamy. Work in all the remaining ingredients until the mixture forms a stiff dough.

3 Divide the mixture into small pieces. Roll them into balls and place on the baking sheets. Press each one flat with a fork. Bake in the preheated oven for 10–12 minutes, until a pale golden brown.

4 Lift off with an offset spatula and cool completely on a wire rack.

5 Store in an airtight container.

MAKING TIME 15 MINUTES
CHILLING TIME 1 HOUR
BAKING TIME 12–15 MINUTES

EASTER BISCUITS

Be sure to use butter for these biscuits as the flavor really does come through.

MAKES ABOUT 24

12 tbsp (6 oz/175g) butter, softened
½ cup (4 oz/100g) superfine sugar, plus extra to glaze
finely grated zest of 1 lemon
2 large egg yolks, plus a little egg white, beaten, to glaze
2 cups (8 oz/225g) all-purpose flour
⅓ cup (1.8 oz/50g) currants

1 Cream the butter with the sugar and lemon zest until light and fluffy. Work in the egg yolks then stir in the flour and currants. Knead lightly until smooth. Leave in the fridge to chill for about 1 hour, until firm.

2 Preheat the oven to 350°F/Convection 320°F and line two baking sheets with nonstick baking paper.

3 Roll out the dough on a lightly floured surface to an ⅛ in thickness and cut into rounds with a fluted 3 in cutter.

4 Lift on to the baking sheets, brush with a little lightly beaten egg white and dredge with sugar. Bake in the preheated oven for 12–15 minutes, until just golden brown.

5 Lift off with an offset spatula and cool completely on a wire rack.

6 Store in an airtight container.

MAKING TIME 10 MINUTES
BAKING TIME 12–15 MINUTES

MEGA PEANUT BUTTER COOKIES

These are great to keep in the cookie jar as they are popular with children. They are easy, too, as they are made with pantry ingredients.

MAKES 24

2 cups (8 oz/225g) self-rising flour
10 tbsp (5 oz/140g) butter, softened
¼ cup (2.2 oz/65g) crunchy peanut butter
½ cup plus 1 tbsp (5 oz/150g) light muscovado sugar
1 large egg, beaten

1 Preheat the oven to 350°F/Convection 320°F and line two large baking sheets with nonstick baking paper.

2 Measure the flour into a bowl and add the butter, peanut butter and sugar. Rub the mixture with your fingertips until it is starting to come together. Add the egg and bring together to form a soft dough.

3 Divide the mixture into 24 pieces, roll them into balls and place, well spaced, on the baking sheets. Press the balls flat with a damp fork. Bake in the preheated oven for 12–15 minutes, until a pale golden brown.

4 Leave on the baking sheet to harden for a few minutes, then lift off with a an offset spatula onto a wire rack to cool.

5 Store in an airtight container.

MAKING TIME 10 MINUTES
BAKING TIME 25 MINUTES

ENGLISH MACAROONS

Rice paper is not always easy to find so you could use nonstick silicone paper instead. Silicone paper is ideal for biscuits with a high sugar content and can be reused many times.

MAKES 16

2 large eggs whites
1¼ cups (5 oz/125g) almond flour
¾ cup (6 oz/175g) superfine sugar
8 blanched almonds, halved

1 Preheat the oven to 350°F/Convection 320°F and line two baking sheets with rice paper or nonstick silicone paper.

2 Set about 1 teaspoonful of the egg white to one side in a small bowl then whisk the remaining egg whites with an electric mixer until they form soft peaks. Fold in the ground almonds and sugar.

3 Place heaped teaspoonfuls of the mixture, well spaced, on the two baking sheets and smooth them out with the back of a spoon to form circles. Place a halved blanched almond in the center of each one. Finally, brush the almonds and tops of the macaroons with a little of the reserved egg white and bake in the preheated oven for about 25 minutes, or until the macaroons are a pale, golden brown.

4 Remove from the oven and leave to cool slightly before lifting from the baking sheets with an offset Spatula. If rice paper has been used, remove any excess paper from around the edges of the macaroons. Cool completely before serving.

MAKING TIME 25 MINUTES
BAKING TIME 8–10 MINUTES

FLORENTINES

I usually have to make double the quantity of these very special biscuits—they disappear so quickly.

MAKES 20

- 4 tbsp (2 oz/55g) butter
- ¼ cup (2 oz/50g) demerara sugar
- 2¾ tbsp (2 oz/55g) golden syrup (available online)
- ½ cup (2 oz/50g) all-prpose flour
- 4 glacé cherries, finely chopped
- ⅓ cup (1.8 oz/50g) currants
- ⅔ cup (2 oz/55g) chopped nuts (such as almonds and walnuts)

For the topping

- 6 oz (175g) bittersweet or semisweet chocolate, melted

1 Preheat the oven to 350°F/Convection 320°F and line three large baking sheets with nonstick baking paper or silicone sheets, or bake in batches.

2 Measure the butter, sugar and syrup into a small pan and heat gently until the butter has melted.

3 Measure the flour, cherries, currants and nuts into a bowl, pour over the melted mixture and stir well until thoroughly mixed.

4 Spoon teaspoonfuls of the mixture onto the prepared baking sheets, leaving plenty of space for them to spread, and bake in the preheated oven for 8–10 minutes, until golden brown.

5 Allow to cool for a few moments, then carefully lift off with an offset spatula and finish cooling on a wire rack. Watch that the Florentines don't become too cool before moving, or they will be difficult to lift off the sheet. If this does happen, put them back in the oven for a minute so they warm through. They will then lift off more easily.

6 When completely cooled, spread a little melted chocolate over the flat base of each Florentine. Mark a zigzag in the chocolate with a fork and leave to set, chocolate-side up, on the wire rack.

7 Store in an airtight container.

MAKING TIME 20 MINUTES
BAKING TIME 10–15 MINUTES

BRANDY SNAPS

The quantities given here result in a lot of brandy snaps, but they keep very well in an airtight container. If only a few are required, it is easy to make half the quantity. They may be served just as they are with ice cream, mousses or soufflés but are also good if you fill them with a little whipped cream and serve them with fruit.

MAKES 30

- ½ cup (4 oz/114g) butter
- ½ cup (4 oz/100g) demerara sugar
- ⅓ cup (4 oz/113g) golden syrup (available online)
- 1 cup (4 oz/100g) all-purpose flour
- 1 level tsp ground ginger
- 1 tsp lemon juice

1 Preheat the oven to 350°F/Convection 320°F, line two or three large baking sheets with nonstick baking paper and oil the handles of four wooden spoons.

2 Measure the butter, sugar and syrup into a heavy-bottomed saucepan and heat gently until the butter and sugar have dissolved—this will take about 15 minutes. Allow the mixture to cool slightly, 2–3 minutes, then sift in the flour and ginger. Stir well, adding the lemon juice. Set aside to cool to room temperature.

3 Place teaspoonfuls of the mixture onto the baking sheets, at least 4 in apart. It is best to put only four spoonfuls on a baking sheet at a time and to bake only one sheet at a time (you will need to work fast once they are baked). Bake in the preheated oven for 10–15 minutes until golden brown.

4 Remove from the oven and leave for a few minutes to firm, then lift from the sheet with an offset spatula. Immediately roll around the wooden spoons and leave to set on a wire rack with the join underneath. Then slip out the spoons. Watch that they don't become too cool before moving, or they will be difficult to lift off the sheet. If this does happen, put them back in the oven for a minute so they warm through. They will then lift off more easily.

5 Store in an airtight container as soon as they are cold; they will keep for at least a week in an airtight container.

MAKING TIME 10 MINUTES
CHILLING TIME 30 MINUTES
BAKING TIME 20 MINUTES

LANCASHIRE BISCUITS

Cheese is always very popular served after a meal, particularly with the male members of the family. I like to have a few of these biscuits stored away in an airtight container to serve with a selection of cheese.

MAKES ABOUT 20

- ½ cup (4 oz/114g) margarine spread
- ⅓ cup (2 oz/50g) semolina
- 1 cup (4 oz/100g) self-rising flour
- 3 oz (75g) mature Lancashire cheese or aged Cheddar, finely grated
- ½ level tsp salt
- ½ level tsp mustard powder
- a generous pinch of cayenne pepper

1 Measure all the ingredients into a large bowl and beat with an electric mixer until well blended and smooth. Knead well, then roll into a sausage shape about 6 in long. Cover in plastic wrap and leave to chill in the fridge for about 30 minutes, until firm.

2 Preheat the oven to 350°F/Convection 320°F and line two baking sheets with nonstick baking paper.

3 Cut the roll into about 20 slices and arrange on the baking sheets. Bake in the preheated oven for about 20 minutes, until golden brown.

4 Leave to cool on the sheets for a few moments, then lift off with an offset spatula and finish cooling on a wire rack.

CHAPTER SEVEN

ESPECIALLY FOR CHILDREN

MAKING TIME 15 MINUTES
BAKING TIME 15–20 MINUTES

JUJUBE CAKES

These tiny cakes are made in petits four paper liners. They are so small that children can eat several at a time, and they seem to enjoy the novelty of them more than a cupcake or bun. My grandchildren enjoy helping to make these, particularly putting the sweets on top.

MAKES ABOUT 24

6 tbsp (3 oz/85g) margarine, from fridge
2 large eggs
1 cup (4 oz/100g) self-rising flour
½ level tsp baking powder
⅓ cup (3 oz/65g) superfine sugar
1 tbsp milk

For the icing

1 cup (4 oz/100g) confectioners' sugar, sifted
about 1 tbsp lemon juice

For the decoration

about 24 Jujubes or jelly beans

1 Preheat the oven to 350°F/Convection 320°F and arrange about 24 petits four liners on a large baking sheet or in mini muffin tins.

2 Measure all the cake ingredients into a bowl and beat well with an electric mixer until thoroughly blended.

3 Spoon teaspoonfuls of the mixture into the liners until they are almost three-quarters full. Be careful not to overfill the liners as the mixture will rise during baking. Bake in the preheated oven for 15–20 minutes, until well risen and pale golden brown.

4 Lift off and cool on wire racks.

5 Measure the confectioners sugar into a bowl and add sufficient lemon juice to give a spreading consistency. Spoon a little on top of each cake and spread out with the back of a teaspoon. When the icing has almost set, top with a Jujube.

MAKING TIME 15 MINUTES
BAKING TIME 10 MINUTES

ICED CUTOUT BISCUITS

My grandchildren adore these. You could use any shapes—stars work well as decorations for the Christmas tree, but you could make rabbits for Easter or any other shapes for a children's party. Let your children be creative—color the icing if you like and have fun with them!

MAKES ABOUT 36

½ cup (4 oz/114g) butter, softened
½ cup (4 oz/100g) superfine sugar
1¾ cups (7 oz/200g) all-purpose flour
2½ tbsp (1 oz/25g) semolina
finely grated zest of 1 lemon
1 large egg, beaten

To decorate

2 cups (8 oz/225g) confectioners' sugar, sifted
food coloring (optional)

1 Preheat the oven to 350°F/Convection 320°F and lightly grease two or three large baking sheets.

2 Measure all the ingredients into a large bowl and beat with an electric mixer until well blended. Turn out onto a lightly floured surface and knead until smooth.

3 Roll out to an ⅛ in thickness, then use your preferred cutter to cut out different shapes. Lift the biscuits onto the baking sheets with an offset spatula, re-roll and cut out the trimmings until all the dough has been used.

4 Bake in the preheated oven for about 10 minutes, until just beginning to tinge with golden brown.

5 Lift off with an offset spatula and cool completely on a wire rack.

6 Measure the confectioners' sugar into a bowl and work in enough water to give a smooth glacé icing, adding coloring as wished. Spread some icing on top of each biscuit to decorate.

MAKING TIME 20 MINUTES
BAKING TIME 15–20 MINUTES

AFGHANS

Everybody's favorites; children love making and eating these.

MAKES 30–35

- 12 tbsp (6 oz/170g) butter, softened
- ½ cup (4 oz/100g) superfine sugar
- 1 cup plus 2 tbsp (5 oz/150g) all-purpose flour
- 2 level tbsp cocoa powder
- 2 cups (1.8 oz/50g) crushed cornflakes

1 Preheat the oven to 350°F/Convection 320°F and grease two or three large baking sheets, or bake in batches.

2 Cream the butter and sugar together until soft then gradually work in the flour, cocoa and, lastly, the crushed cornflakes.

3 Shape the mixture into small balls the size of a walnut and place, well spaced, on the baking sheets. Press each ball down with two fingers. Bake in the preheated oven for 15–20 minutes.

4 Lift off with an offset spatula and cool completely on a wire rack. Store in an airtight container.

MAKING TIME 15 MINUTES
BAKING TIME 25 MINUTES

CRUNCHIES

Children adore these crunchies, and it's nice to include a couple in a packed lunch.

MAKES 20

½ cup (4 oz/114g) margarine, from fridge
⅓ cup (3 oz/75g) superfine sugar
1 large egg yolk
1 cup plus 2 tbsp (5 oz/150g) self-raising flour
about 1 cup (1 oz/25g) Rice Krispies

1 Heat the oven to 350°F/Convection 320°F and line two large baking sheets with nonstick baking paper.

2 Measure all the ingredients except the Rice Krispies into a bowl and work together using a wooden spoon until well mixed and smooth.

3 Take heaped teaspoonfuls of the mixture and roll into 20 balls. Roll each one in the Rice Krispies and arrange well spaced on the baking sheets. Slightly flatten each one and bake in the preheated oven for about 25 minutes, until just beginning to color at the edges.

4 Leave to cool on the sheets for a few moments, then lift off with an offset spatula and finish cooling on a wire rack.

MAKING TIME 10 MINUTES
CHILLING TIME 6 HOURS

TRAFFIC LIGHTS

These are very easy to make and are ideal for a children's party.

MAKES 8

- 6 oz (175g) bittersweet or semisweet chocolate
- 3 oz (75g) graham crackers, roughly crushed
- ½ × 14 oz (396g) can full-fat condensed milk
- red, yellow and green glacé cherries, halved

1 Grease a 7 in square cake tin and line with nonstick baking paper.

2 Break the chocolate into small pieces and melt in a heatproof bowl over a pan of hot water. Stir occasionally until quite smooth.

3 Remove from the heat and stir in the biscuits and condensed milk. Turn into the tin and smooth flat with the back of a spoon.

4 Refrigerate for about 6 hours, until set.

5 Cut into 8 bars and decorate with the halved cherries in a traffic light pattern.

MAKING TIME 10–15 MINUTES
CHILLING TIME 6 HOURS

CAROLINE'S CHOCOLATE SLAB

This is very popular with all my family and is an ideal recipe for children to make on their own. Any plain biscuits will do for this; it is a good way of using up the broken pieces from the bottom of the cookie jar.

MAKES 16

- 6 oz (175g) plain digestive biscuits or graham crackers
- ½ cup (4 oz/100g) superfine sugar
- ½ cup (4 oz/114g) butter
- 4 oz (100g) bittersweet or semisweet chocolate
- ⅓ cup (1.8 oz/50g) sultanas

1 Line a 7 in square cake tin with plastic wrap.

2 Put the biscuits in a plastic bag and crush with a rolling pin into small pieces.

3 Measure the sugar and butter into a pan and heat over low until the butter has melted.

4 Remove the pan from the heat and stir in the chocolate until melted. Add the crushed biscuits and sultanas and mix well.

5 Press the mixture into the tin and smooth the top. Leave to chill in the fridge for about 6 hours, until set.

6 Cut into 16 squares and store in an airtight container.

MAKING TIME 10 MINUTES
CHILLING TIME 6 HOURS

PEANUT SQUARES

These are easy to make and could be made by children. Use any broken biscuits that have accumulated at the bottom of the cookie jar.

MAKES 16

- 6 tbsp (3 oz/85g) butter
- ¼ cup (2 oz/50g) light muscovado sugar
- 4 tbsp golden syrup (available online)
- 4 tbsp crunchy peanut butter
- 6 oz (175g) graham crackers, lightly crushed

1 Wet a 7 in square cake tin with water, then line with a piece of plastic wrap.

2 Place the butter in a small pan with the sugar and syrup and bring slowly to a boil, stirring until the sugar has dissolved and the butter has melted.

3 Remove from the heat and stir in the peanut butter. Finally, add the biscuits and mix well.

4 Press the mixture into the tin and press down firmly. Leave to chill in the fridge for about 6 hours, until set quite firm.

5 Cut into 16 squares and store in an airtight container.

MAKING TIME 15 MINUTES
CHILLING TIME 6 HOURS

MARSHMALLOW SLICES

When the children are home from school on vacation and are fed up with amusing themselves, encourage them to bake! They love to have something to show for their time and effort.

MAKES 16

- ½ cup (4 oz/114g) butter
- 3 tbsp golden syrup (available online)
- ¼ cup (1 oz/25g) drinking chocolate
- 8 oz (225g) digestive biscuits or graham crackers, crumbled
- 8 regular-sized marshmallows, snipped into small pieces with wet scissors

For the topping

- 4½ oz (125g) bittersweet or semisweet chocolate, melted

1 Wet a 7 in square cake tin and line with plastic wrap.

2 Measure the butter, syrup and drinking chocolate into a large pan over low heat and stir gently until the butter has melted.

3 Remove from the heat and allow to cool slightly before stirring in the biscuits and marshmallows. Mix well until thoroughly blended.

4 Turn the mixture into the tin and level the top. Press down firmly with the back of a spoon and refrigerate for about 6 hours, until firm.

5 Spread this biscuit base with the melted chocolate, then leave for another hour to set.

6 Peel off the plastic wrap and cut into squares to serve.

MAKING TIME 10–15 MINUTES
BAKING TIME 35–40 MINUTES

CHOCOLATE CHIP BARS

These crunchy bars are a hot favorite in our house. They are very easy to make because everything is put into one bowl.

MAKES 16

½ cup (4 oz/114g) butter, softened
½ cup plus 1 tbsp (5 oz/150g) demerara sugar
1 large egg
1 tsp vanilla extract
2 cups (8 oz/225g) self-rising flour
½ cup (4 oz/100g) semisweet chocolate chips

1 Preheat the oven to 375°F/Convection 325°F and grease an 11 x 7 in Swiss roll tin.

2 Measure all the ingredients into a bowl and mix thoroughly. If you find it easier, use your hands.

3 Spread the mixture into the tin and bake in the preheated oven for 35–40 minutes, until golden brown and shrinking slightly from the sides of the tin.

4 Leave to cool slightly then cut into 16 pieces.

5 Lift out and leave to finish cooling on a wire rack.

MAKING TIME 10 MINUTES
SETTING TIME 1 HOUR

CHOCOLATE KRISPIES

Make sure the Krispies are mixed really well so that they are thoroughly coated with the chocolate mixture.

MAKES 15

- ½ cup (4 oz/114g) butter
- 3 rounded tbsp golden syrup (available online)
- 1 level tbsp cocoa powder
- 1 oz (25g) bittersweet or semisweet chocolate
- 3 cups (3 oz/75g) Rice Krispies

1 Arrange 15 cupcake liners on a large baking sheet.

2 Melt the butter and syrup in a small pan over a gentle heat. Add the cocoa and chocolate. Remove from the heat and stir until melted.

3 Add the Krispies and mix very thoroughly until they are well coated.

4 Spoon into the liners and leave to harden in a cool room for about 1 hour.

MAKING TIME 25 MINUTES
SETTING TIME 30 MINUTES

TOFFEE AND CHOCOLATE KRISPIE SQUARES

These are delicious. They take a little time to make but are really worth the effort.

MAKES 16

6 tbsp (3 oz/85g) butter
½ cup plus 1 tbsp (5 oz/150g) granulated sugar
1 tbsp golden syrup (available online)
1 × 14 oz (396g) can full-fat condensed milk
4 cups (4 oz/100g) Rice Krispies

For the topping

4 oz (100g) bittersweet or semisweet chocolate, melted

1 Lightly grease a 7 in square cake tin and line with nonstick baking paper.

2 Measure the butter, sugar, syrup and condensed milk into a heavy-bottomed saucepan and heat gently until the sugar has dissolved and the butter has melted. Bring slowly to the boil and simmer for 20 minutes, until thick and a rich caramel color. Stir continuously and scrape the bottom and sides of the pan, otherwise the mixture will catch.

3 Remove from the heat and drop a little of the mixture into cold water. If it hardens it is ready. Stir in the Rice Krispies to coat them well.

4 Tip the mixture into the tin and pack down. Work quickly as it will harden.

5 Pour over the melted chocolate and spread to cover completely.

6 Leave to cool until set.

7 When completely cool, cut into 16 squares and store in an airtight container.

SANDWICHES

MAKING TIME 10 MINUTES
SETTING TIME 30 MINUTES

CHOCOLATE AND SULTANA CLUSTERS

These are most children's all-time favorites. For best results they should be eaten on the day they are made—this is usually no problem! Let the children make them themselves and try to persuade them that it is worth waiting for the clusters to set.

MAKES 12

- 4 tbsp (2 oz/55g) butter
- 1 rounded tbsp golden syrup (available online)
- 3 oz (75g) bittersweet or semisweet chocolate, broken into pieces
- 3 cups (3 oz/75g) cornflakes
- ⅓ cup (1.8 oz/50g) sultanas

1 Arrange 12 paper liners on a large baking sheet.

2 Measure the butter and syrup into a saucepan and heat over low until melted.

3 Remove from the heat and stir in the chocolate. Mix well until melted.

4 Tip in all the cornflakes and sultanas and stir very well so they become evenly coated with the chocolate mixture.

5 Using two spoons, pile the mixture into the liners and then leave to harden in a cool room for about 30 minutes.

MAKING TIME 10 MINUTES
SETTING TIME 1–2 HOURS

ANNABEL'S CARAMEL BARS

Children love to eat these bars instead of cakes or biscuits; I find they are also very popular accompaniments to ice cream. You can cut down the recipe and make only half the quantity, but in our house they are so popular and useful that it never seems worthwhile to make less.

MAKES 21

½ cup (4 oz/114g) butter
16 regular-sized marshmallows
4 oz (100g) toffee candies
7 cups (7 oz/200g) Rice Krispies

1 You will need a 12 x 9 in traybake tin.

2 Measure the butter, marshmallows and toffee candies into a saucepan and heat over medium until melted and smooth. Be patient, this will take about 5 minutes.

3 Meanwhile, measure the Krispies into a large bowl.

4 Remove the pan from the heat and pour all at once onto the Krispies. Stir very thoroughly until they are evenly coated.

5 Spoon into the tin and press flat with the back of a spoon. Leave in a cool place for 1–2 hours until set.

6 Cut into 21 bars.

MAKING TIME 20 MINUTES
CHILLING TIME 1 HOUR
BAKING TIME 12–15 MINUTES

HAPPY FACE BISCUITS

This biscuit recipe can be used in a variety of ways—use different shapes or add your own flavorings.

MAKES ABOUT 24

- 12 tbsp (6 oz/170g) butter, softened
- ½ cup (4 oz/100g) superfine sugar, plus extra to sprinkle
- finely grated zest of 1 lemon
- 2 large egg yolks, plus a little egg white to glaze
- 2 cups (8 oz/225g) all-purpose flour
- about 2/3 cup (4 oz/100g) currants

1 Cream the butter with the sugar until light and fluffy. Gradually work in the lemon zest, egg yolks and flour. Knead until smooth then wrap in plastic wrap and leave to chill in the fridge for about 1 hour, until firm.

2 Preheat the oven to 350°F/Convection 320°F and line two large baking sheets with nonstick baking paper.

3 Roll out the dough to ⅛ in thickness and cut into rounds with a 3 in cutter.

4 Arrange the biscuits on the prepared baking sheets and use the currants to make a happy face on each one. Brush with a little egg white, sprinkle with a little sugar and bake in the preheated oven for 12–15 minutes until pale golden brown.

5 Leave to cool on the sheets for a few moments, then lift off with an offset spatula and finish cooling on a wire rack.

MAKING TIME 15 MINUTES
SETTING TIME 1–2 HOURS

COCONUT ICE

This is an easy, no-cook recipe that children can make on their own.

MAKES 36

- ¾ cup (6 oz/175ml) full-fat condensed milk
- 3 cups (12 oz/350g) confectioners' sugar
- 3 cups (6.3 oz/180g) desiccated coconut
- a few drops red food coloring

1 Lightly grease a 7 in square tin.

2 Measure the condensed milk, confectioners' sugar and coconut together into a large bowl and mix very thoroughly until the mixture comes together and can be lightly kneaded to a smooth ball.

3 Press half of the mixture evenly over the base of the tin.

4 Add some red coloring to the remaining mixture in the bowl. It is surprising how much will be needed to make a good pink color—the best way to add the color is to drip it, drop by drop, from a skewer dipped in the red coloring. Work each addition thoroughly into the mixture to make sure that the pink is a uniform color throughout.

5 Press the pink mixture on top of the white mixture and leave in a cool place to set for 1–2 hours, preferably overnight.

6 Cut into 36 squares and store in an airtight container.

MAKING TIME 10 MINUTES
BAKING TIME 40–45 MINUTES

COCONUT CRACKERJACKS

These are similar to flapjacks, but the addition of coconut gives a crisp texture that is always popular.

MAKES 18

- 10 tbsp (5 oz/140g) margarine, from fridge
- ½ cup plus 1 tbsp (5 oz/150g) demerara sugar
- 1½ cups (5.3 oz/150g) rolled oats
- ½ cup (1 oz/25g) desiccated coconut

1 Preheat the oven to 320°F/Convection 270°F and grease a 11 × 7 in Swiss roll tin.

2 Cream the spread and sugar together, then add the oats and coconut and work the mixture together.

3 Press this into the tin and bake in the preheated oven for 40–45 minutes, until golden brown.

4 Leave to cool in the tin for about 10 minutes, then mark into 18 squares or fingers. Finish cooling in the tin.

5 Lift out and store in an airtight container.

MAKING TIME 5 MINUTES
BAKING TIME 30–35 MINUTES

SULTANA FLAPJACKS

These are simple and quick to make from ingredients that are in the cupboard. Most children find them very easy both to make and eat!

MAKES 16

12 tbsp (6 oz/170g) butter
½ cup (4 oz/125g) demerara sugar
2¾ tbsp (2 oz/50g) golden syrup (available online)
2 cups (7.1 oz/200g) rolled oats
½ cup (2.6 oz/75g) sultanas

1 Preheat the oven to 350°F/Confection 320°F. Grease a shallow, 7 in square tin and line with nonstick baking paper.

2 Measure the butter, sugar and syrup into a small pan and heat gently over a low heat until the butter has melted.

3 Remove from the heat and stir in the oats and sultanas. Mix well, then turn into the tin and press flat.

4 Bake in the preheated oven for 30–35 minutes, or until pale golden brown.

5 Remove from the oven and leave for 10 minutes. Mark into 16 fingers, then leave to finish cooling in the tin.

6 Lift out and store in an airtight container.

MAKING TIME 10 MINUTES
BAKING TIME 30–35 MINUTES

CHEWY ALMOND FLAPJACKS

A very dear lady in the village gave me this recipe. I tried it at home and it was a hit with the family.

MAKES 16

1 cup (8 oz/225g) butter
½ cup plus 1 tbsp (7 oz/200g) golden syrup (available online)
½ cup (4 oz/100g) demerara sugar
2 cups (7 oz/200g) porridge oats (Scottish oatmeal)
1 cup (4 oz/100g) slivered almonds

1 Preheat the oven to 350°F/Convection 320°F. Grease a 7 in square tin and line with nonstick baking paper.

2 Measure the butter, syrup and sugar into a small pan and heat gently over a low until the butter has melted.

3 Measure the oats and slivered almonds into a large bowl and pour the melted mixture over the top. Stir well until thoroughly mixed.

4 Spread evenly into the tin and bake in the preheated oven for 30–35 minutes, or until golden brown.

5 Remove from the oven and mark into 16 squares. Cool completely in the tin.

6 Lift out and store in an airtight container.

MAKING TIME 10 MINUTES
BAKING TIME 20–25 MINUTES

ORANGE MARSHMALLOW CAKE

Marshmallows give a lovely topping to this cake. Arrange them on the top as soon as it comes out of the oven so that they soften and stick to the cake then, when cold, pour over the icing.

SERVES 8

½ cup (4 oz/114g) margarine, from fridge
½ cup (4 oz/100g) superfine caster sugar
1 cup (4 oz/100g) self-rising flour
½ level tsp baking powder
2 large eggs
finely grated zest of 1 orange

For the topping

about 3 cups (3 oz/75g) mini marshmallows

For the icing

1½ cups (6 oz/175g) confectioners' sugar, sifted
about 3 tbsp orange juice, warmed

1 Preheat the oven to 350°F/Convection 320°F. Grease an 8 in loose-bottomed cake or springform tin and line with nonstick baking paper.

2 Measure all the cake ingredients into a bowl and beat with an electric mixer until light, fluffy and well blended.

3 Turn the mixture into the tin, level the top and bake in the preheated oven for 20–25 minutes, or until well risen and golden brown. The cake will have shrunk slightly from the sides of the tin and the top will spring back when pressed with a finger.

4 Remove the cake from the oven and place the marshmallows over the top. Cool completely in the tin.

5 Meanwhile, blend the confectioners' sugar and orange juice together.

6 Lift the cake from the tin, remove the paper and place on a serving plate. Pour the icing over the top just before serving—the icing will run away into any cracks in the marshmallow topping and slightly down the sides.

MAKING TIME 20 MINUTES
BAKING TIME 10–15 MINUTES

JAMMY BUNS

I asked a 12-year-old girl to try this recipe for me—she had no problems and thoroughly enjoyed herself. The buns are best eaten fresh from the oven.

MAKES 12

2 cups (8 oz/225g) self-rising flour
¼ level tsp pumpkin pie spice
4 tbsp (2 oz/55g) butter
¼ cup (2 oz/50g) superfine sugar
1 large egg, beaten
about 2 tbsp milk
about 2 tbsp strawberry jam
a little granulated sugar

1 Preheat the oven to 400°F/Convection 350°F and line a large baking sheet with nonstick baking paper.

2 Measure the flour and spice into a bowl and rub in the butter until the mixture resembles fine breadcrumbs. Stir in the sugar.

3 Blend the egg with the milk then stir into the mixture, adding sufficient liquid to make a stiff dough.

4 Divide into 12 pieces and roll into balls. Make a hole in the center of each ball with the handle of a wooden spoon—wiggle it about a bit to make the hole as big as possible. Measure about ½ teaspoon of jam into each hole then pinch the opening firmly to close together.

5 Turn the buns over and place them, sealed-side down, on the baking sheets. Sprinkle with a little granulated sugar and bake in the preheated oven for 10–15 minutes, or until pale golden brown.

6 Lift off with an offset spatula and place on a wire rack. Serve warm.

MAKING TIME 15 MINUTES
BAKING TIME 3 MINUTES

BAKED ALASKA BIRTHDAY CAKE

When I made this for Annabel's birthday cake a few years ago, instead of candles I served it with a sparkler burning in the top. She and all her friends thought it was wonderful.

SERVES 8

- 1 Swiss Roll (store-bought or see page 36)
- about 8 scoops raspberry ripple ice cream (not the soft-scoop type)
- 4 large egg whites
- 1 cup (8 oz/225g) superfine sugar

1 Cut the Swiss roll into 8 slices and arrange in a round on an ovenproof plate. Pile the scoops of ice cream on top of the Swiss roll and put in the freezer while making the meringue.

2 Place the egg whites in a large bowl and beat on high speed with an electric mixer until soft peaks form.

3 Add the sugar, a generous teaspoonful at a time, beating well after each addition, until all the sugar has been added.

4 Take the cake from the freezer and spread the meringue all over so that the ice cream is completely sealed inside. Return to the freezer until required. It will keep in the freezer at this stage for up to 1 week.

5 To serve, heat the oven to 450°F/Convection 400°F and bake the cake for about 3 minutes, until just tinged golden brown. Serve immediately.

CHAPTER EIGHT

TEA BREADS AND SCONES

MAKING TIME 10 MINUTES
BAKING TIME 2 HOURS

FARMHOUSE FRUIT LOAF

A fruit cake baked in a loaf tin—very easy to cut for serving and packing in a lunch box.

SERVES 10

- 2 cups (8 oz/225g) self-rising flour
- 2 oz (50g) glacé cherries, quartered, rinsed and thoroughly dried
- 12 tbsp (6 oz/170g) margarine or softened butter
- ½ cup plus 2 tbsp (6 oz/175g) light muscovado sugar
- 3 large eggs
- 2 tbsp milk
- 1 cup (5.3 oz/150g) seedless raisins
- 1 cup (5.3 oz/150g) sultanas

1 Preheat the oven to 320°F/Convection 270°F. Grease a 9 × 5 in (2 lb) loaf tin and line with nonstick baking paper.

2 Measure all the ingredients into a bowl and beat thoroughly until well blended.

3 Turn the mixture into the tin, level the top and bake in the preheated oven for about 2 hours, or until a skewer inserted into the center of the loaf comes out clean.

4 Leave to cool in the tin for 10 minutes, then turn out and cool completely on a wire rack.

MAKING TIME 5 MINUTES
BAKING TIME 50–60 MINUTES

FRUIT MALT LOAF

This loaf is so easy (and so good) that I am sure children could make it. All the ingredients are likely to be on hand in your pantry. Serve the loaf sliced, spread with butter.

SERVES 8–10

- 1¼ cups (6 oz/175g) self-rising flour
- 2 level tbsp Ovaltine malt drink powder
- 2¼ tbsp (1 oz/25g) superfine or light muscovado sugar
- ½ cup (2.6 oz/75g) sultanas
- 2 tbsp golden syrup (available online)
- ⅔ cup (5 oz/150ml) milk

1 Preheat the oven to 350°F/Convection 320°F. Grease an 8½ × 4½ in (1 lb) loaf tin and line with nonstick baking paper.

2 Measure all the ingredients into a large bowl and beat thoroughly until well blended.

3 Turn the mixture into the tin and bake in the preheated oven for 50–60 minutes, or until a skewer inserted into the centre of the loaf comes out clean.

4 Turn out and cool completely on a wire rack.

MAKING TIME 10 MINUTES
BAKING TIME 1 HOUR

OLD ENGLISH SEED CAKE

Seed cakes were always popular in the past; this one is a more updated version.

SERVES 8

- 12 tbsp (6 oz/170g) margarine, from fridge
- ½ cup (4 oz/100g) superfine sugar
- 2 large eggs
- 2 cups (8 oz/225g) self-rising flour
- 1 level tsp baking powder
- 1 rounded tbsp caraway seeds
- finely grated zest of 1 lemon
- 4 tbsp milk

1 Preheat the oven to 350°F/Convection 320°F. Grease a deep, 7 in round cake tin and line with nonstick baking paper.

2 Measure all the ingredients into a bowl and beat with an electric mixer until well blended.

3 Turn the mixture into the tin, level the top and bake in the preheated oven for about 1 hour, until well risen and shrinking from the sides of the tin. A skewer inserted into the center of the cake should come out clean.

4 Leave to cool in the tin for about 10 minutes, then turn out, remove the paper and finish cooling on a wire rack.

SOAKING TIME OVERNIGHT
MAKING TIME 15 MINUTES
BAKING TIME 1 HOUR

YORKSHIRE TEA BREAD

This tea bread is quick to make and will keep for up to two weeks in an airtight container. Serve sliced, spread with unsalted butter.

SERVES 10

- 1¼ cups (8 oz/225g) mixed dried fruit
- ¾ cup (6 oz/180ml) cold strained black tea
- ½ cup (4 oz/100g) dark soft brown sugar
- 2 cups (8 oz/225g) self-rising flour
- 2 large eggs

1 Soak the mixed fruit overnight in the tea in a large bowl, covered with a plate. If this is not possible, put the fruit in hot tea and leave for several hours, until the fruit soaks up most of the liquid.

2 Preheat the oven to 320°F/Convection 270°F. Grease a 9 × 5 in (2 lb) loaf tin and line with nonstick baking paper.

3 Add the remaining ingredients to the fruit and beat until well blended.

4 Pour into the tin and bake in the preheated oven for about 1 hour, or until a skewer inserted into the center of the tea bread comes out clean.

5 Leave to cool in the tin, then turn out to cool completely on a wire rack.

MAKING TIME 10 MINUTES
BAKING TIME 1¼ HOURS

HONEY LOAF

This loaf is very good if it is served thinly sliced and spread with unsalted butter.

SERVES 12

¾ cup (2 oz/50g) mixed candied citrus peel
3 cups (12 oz/350g) self-rising flour
1 level tbsp pumpkin pie spice
½ cup (4 oz/100g) soft brown sugar
½ cup (6 oz/170g) clear honey
⅔ cup (5 oz/150ml) milk
about 8 sugar cubes, crushed

1 Preheat the oven to 350°F/Convection 320°F. Grease a 9 × 5 in (2 lb) loaf tin and line with nonstick baking paper.

2 Chop the peel very finely and place in a bowl with the flour, spice and brown sugar and stir until well blended. Make a well in the center, stir in the honey and milk and blend until a smooth, stiff dough is formed.

3 Turn into the tin, sprinkle the crushed sugar cubes over the top of the loaf then bake in the preheated oven for about 1¼ hours. The loaf should be shrinking from the sides of the tin and a skewer inserted into the center should come out clean.

4 Turn out, remove the paper and cool completely on a wire rack.

MAKING TIME 10 MINUTES
BAKING TIME 1 HOUR

ORANGE AND WALNUT LOAF

Serve this loaf in slices, alone or spread with butter. For a change add currants instead of the candied peel, and lemon zest and juice instead of the orange. Both combinations are delicious.

SERVES 8–10

- 1½ cups (6 oz/175g) self-rising flour
- ¾ level tsp baking powder
- finely grated zest and juice of 1 large orange
- ½ cup (2.2 oz/65g) walnuts, chopped
- ¾ cup (2 oz/50g) candied citrus peel, chopped
- 6 tbsp (3 oz/85g) margarine, from fridge
- ⅓ cup (3 oz/75g) light muscovado sugar
- 1 large egg, beaten
- 3 tbsp milk

1 Preheat the oven to 350°F/Convection 320°F. Grease an 8½ × 4½ in (1 lb) loaf tin and line with nonstick baking paper.

2 Measure all the ingredients into a large bowl and beat well until thoroughly blended.

3 Turn into the tin and bake in the preheated oven for about 1 hour, or until well risen. A skewer inserted into the center of the loaf should come out clean.

4 Leave to cool in the tin for about 15 minutes, then turn out, remove the paper and cool completely on a wire rack.

MAKING TIME 20 MINUTES
BAKING TIME 45 MINUTES

MILD GINGER LOAF

This is very easy to make. I often have candied ginger left on the shelf after Christmas, and this is one of my favorite ways of using it up. Best to eat within 2 days of baking. This is lovely served in slices with butter.

SERVES 10–12

- ½ cup (4 oz/114g) margarine, from fridge
- ½ cup (4 oz/100g) light muscovado sugar
- 2 tbsp black molasses
- 2 cups (8 oz/225g) self-rising flour
- 1 level tsp baking powder
- 1 level tsp ground ginger
- ¼ cup (2 oz/55g) candied ginger, well drained and chopped
- 2 large eggs

1 Preheat the oven to 320°F/Convection 270°F. Grease a 9 × 5 in (2 lb) loaf tin and line with nonstick baking paper.

2 Measure the baking spread, sugar and molasses into a pan and heat over low until the spread has melted.

3 Put all the dry ingredients in a bowl, add the melted mixture, the chopped ginger and eggs and beat well for a minute until thoroughly blended.

4 Pour into the tin and bake in the preheated oven for about 45 minutes, or until well risen. A skewer inserted into the center of the loaf should come out clean.

5 Leave to cool in the tin for about 5 minutes, then turn out, remove the paper and cool completely on a wire rack.

MAKING TIME 15 MINUTES
BAKING TIME 45 MINUTES

GINGERBREAD

Chopped candied ginger gives this gingerbread a very special flavor and the finished cake looks delicious if it is iced with a simple lemon icing and decorated with small pieces of crystallized lemon.

MAKES 12 SQUARES

- 1½ cups (4 oz/175g) all-purpose flour
- ¾ level tsp baking powder
- 2 level tsp ground ginger
- 4 tbsp (2 oz/55g) margarine, from fridge
- ¼ cup (2 oz/50g) light muscovado sugar
- 1 tbsp black molasses
- 1 tbsp golden syrup (available online)
- 1 level tsp baking soda
- ¾ cup (6 oz/180ml) warm milk
- 2 large eggs
- 3 tbsp (1½ oz/40g) candied ginger, finely chopped

1 Preheat the oven to 320°F/Convection 270°F. Grease an 8 in square cake tin and line with nonstick baking paper.

2 Sift the flour, baking powder and ground ginger into a bowl.

3 Cream the spread and sugar together with the molasses and syrup in a large bowl and beat very well.

4 Dissolve the baking soda in the warm milk then stir into the creamed sugary mixture. Add the flour mixture, the eggs and candied ginger and beat well until thoroughly blended.

5 Turn into the tin and bake in the preheated oven for about 45 minutes, or until the gingerbread is risen and firm to the touch.

6 Leave to cool in the tin.

MAKING TIME 20 MINUTES
BAKING TIME 1 HOUR

CHOCOLATE AND ORANGE LOAF

This is quite a shallow loaf but is beautifully moist and can be eaten happily without any butter.

SERVES 10–12

- 12 tbsp (6 oz/170g) margarine, from fridge
- ¾ cup (6 oz/175g) superfine sugar
- 1½ cups (6 oz/175g) self-rising flour
- ¾ level tsp baking powder
- finely grated zest of 1 orange
- 3 large eggs
- 2 tbsp milk

For the icing

- 4 tbsp (2 oz/55g) butter
- ¼ cup (1 oz/25g) cocoa powder, sifted
- 2–3 tbsp orange juice
- 1 cup (4 oz/100g) confectioners' sugar, sifted

1 Preheat the oven to 375°F/Convection 325°F. Grease a 9 × 5 in (2 lb) loaf tin and line with nonstick baking paper.

2 Measure all the ingredients for the loaf into a large bowl and beat with an electric mixer until well blended.

3 Turn the mixture into the tin and bake in the preheated oven for about 1 hour until well risen and the top springs back when lightly pressed with a finger.

4 Leave to cool in the tin, then turn out and remove the paper.

5 To make the icing, measure the butter, cocoa, orange juice and confectioners' sugar into a bowl. Beat well to a light, smooth consistency.

6 Spread the icing evenly over the top of the loaf and serve in slices.

SOAKING TIME OVERNIGHT
MAKING TIME 5 MINUTES
BAKING TIME 1½ HOURS

ROUND ORANGE TEA BREAD

A simple tea bread with a lovely orange flavor. Prepare it in the afternoon with the remains of the tea, leave to stand overnight and then make the bread the following morning.

SERVES 10

- 1 cup (5.2 oz/150g) currants
- 1 cup (5.2 oz/150g) seedless raisins
- 1¼ cups (5 oz/150g) light muscovado sugar
- finely grated zest of 2 oranges
- 1¼ cups (10 oz/300ml) hot black tea
- 2½ cups (10 oz/275g) self-rising flour
- 1 large egg, beaten

1 Put the fruit, sugar and orange zest in a bowl and pour in the hot tea. Stir very well, cover with a plate to keep the heat in and then leave to stand overnight.

2 Preheat the oven to 300°F/Convection 250°F. Grease an 8 in round cake tin and line with nonstick baking paper.

3 Stir the flour and egg into the soaked fruit and mix very well.

4 Turn the mixture into the tin and bake in the preheated oven for about 1½ hours, or until the tea bread is shrinking from the sides of the tin. A skewer inserted into the center should come out clean.

5 Turn out, remove the paper and cool completely on a wire rack.

6 Serve sliced, either spread with butter or just as it is.

SOAKING TIME OVERNIGHT
MAKING TIME 5 MINUTES
BAKING TIME 2 HOURS

ALL-BRAN TEA BREAD LOAF

Soak the fruit overnight so that it plumps up and the next day all that is necessary is to stir the remaining ingredients into the mixture. It is a very easy loaf to make and the finished result has a lovely flavor. Serve sliced and spread with butter or just as it is.

SERVES 10

2¼ cups (12 oz/350g) dried fruit
1 cup (8 oz/225g) demerara sugar
1¼ cups (10 oz/300ml) cold black tea
1¼ cups (5 oz/105g) self-rising flour
3 cups (5.1 oz/150g) All-Bran
1 large egg, beaten

1 Put the fruit and sugar in a bowl and pour over the tea. Stir well, then leave to stand overnight.

2 Preheat the oven to 300°F/Convection 250°F. Grease a 9 × 5 in (2 lb) loaf tin and line with nonstick baking paper.

3 Stir the flour, All-Bran and egg into the fruit and mix very thoroughly.

4 Turn the mixture into the tin and bake in the preheated oven for about 2 hours, or until the mixture has risen slightly and shrinks away from the sides of the tin. A skewer inserted into the center should come out clean.

5 Turn out and leave to cool on a wire rack.

MAKING TIME 5 MINUTES
BAKING TIME 40–45 MINUTES

QUICK CHERRY LOAF

Be sure to wash and dry the glacé cherries thoroughly, otherwise they do have a tendency to sink!

SERVES 8–10

- 4 oz (100g) glacé cherries, chopped, rinsed and thoroughly dried
- 1 cup (4 oz/100g) self-rising flour
- ½ cup (4 oz/114g) margarine, from fridge
- ½ cup (4 oz/100g) superfine sugar
- 2 large eggs
- finely grated zest of 1 small orange
- 2½ tbsp (1 oz/25g) semolina

1 Preheat the oven to 350°F/Convection 320°F. Grease an 8½ × 4½ in (1 lb) loaf tin and line with nonstick baking paper.

2 Measure all the ingredients into a large bowl and beat well until thoroughly blended.

3 Turn the mixture into the tin, level the top and bake in the preheated oven for 40–45 minutes, or until well risen. A skewer inserted into the center of the loaf should come out clean.

4 Leave to cool in the tin for a few minutes, then turn out, remove the paper and cool completely on a wire rack.

5 Serve in slices.

MAKING TIME 10 MINUTES
BAKING TIME 1½ HOURS

BANANA LOAF

A delicious cut-and-come-again loaf that really tastes of banana.

SERVES 10

- 2 ripe bananas, mashed down with a fork
- 1 cup (4 oz/100g) whole-wheat flour
- 1¼ cups (5 oz/150g) self-rising flour
- 1 level tsp baking powder
- ½ cup (4 oz/114g) margarine, from fridge
- ¾ cup (6 oz/175g) light muscovado sugar
- 2 large eggs
- ½ cup plus 2 tbsp (5.3 oz/150g) plain yogurt
- 1 cup (5.2 oz/150g) currants
- 2 tbsp milk

1 Preheat the oven to 350°F/Convection 320°F. Grease a 9 × 5 in (2 lb) loaf tin and line with nonstick baking paper.

2 Measure all the ingredients into a large bowl and beat well until thoroughly blended.

3 Turn into the tin and bake in the preheated oven for about 1½ hours, or until well risen. A skewer inserted into the center of the loaf should come out clean.

4 Leave to cool in the tin for about 15 minutes, then turn out, remove the paper and cool completely on a wire rack.

5 Serve in slices with butter.

MAKING TIME 10 MINUTES
BAKING TIME 40 MINUTES

NORTH-COUNTRY PARKIN

Store for at least a week before eating in order to allow time for the molasses flavor to develop fully.

MAKES 16 PIECES

3¾ cups (12 oz/350g) stone-ground oatmeal
1½ cups (6 oz/175g) all-purpose flour
1 level tbsp superfine sugar
½ level tsp ground ginger
½ cup (4 oz/114g) margarine, from fridge
1⅓ cups (1 lb/450g) black molasses
5 tbsp milk
½ level tsp baking soda

1 Preheat the oven to 375°F/Convection 325°F. Grease the base of a 12 x 9 in traybake tin and line with nonstick baking paper.

2 Measure the oatmeal, flour, sugar and ginger into a large bowl.

3 Measure the margarine and molasses into a pan and heat gently until the spread has melted.

4 Warm the milk in a separate pan and stir in the baking soda until dissolved. Add to the molasses mixture.

5 Make a well in the center of the dry ingredients and stir in the wet ingredients. Mix very well until thoroughly blended.

6 Turn the mixture into the tin and bake in the preheated oven for about 40 minutes, or until the parkin is shrinking away from the sides of the tin. A skewer inserted into the center of the parkin should come out clean.

7 Turn out and cool completely on a wire rack.

8 When cooled, cut into 16 pieces. Store for a week in an airtight container before serving.

SOAKING TIME OVERNIGHT
MAKING TIME 5 MINUTES
BAKING TIME 1¾ HOURS

WELSH CURRANT LOAF

This loaf lasts extremely well, especially if kept covered in plastic wrap.

SERVES 10–12

- 1 cup (5.2 oz/175g) currants
- 1 cup (5.2 oz/175g) sultanas
- 1 cup (8 oz/225g) light muscovado sugar
- 1⅓ cups (10 oz/300ml) cider
- 1¼ cups (5 oz/150g) self-rising flour
- 1¼ cups (5 oz/150g) whole-wheat flour
- 1 level tsp baking powder
- 1 large egg, beaten

1 Measure the fruits and sugar into a large bowl, pour over the cider and leave to stand overnight covered with plastic wrap.

2 Preheat the oven to 300°F/Convection 250°F. Grease a 9 × 5 in (2 lb) loaf tin and line with nonstick baking paper.

3 Stir the flours, baking powder and egg into the fruit mixture and beat well until thoroughly blended.

4 Turn the mixture into the tin and level the top. Bake in the preheated oven for about 1¾ hours, or until well risen. A skewer inserted into the center of the loaf should come out clean.

5 Leave to cool in the tin for a few minutes, then turn out, remove the paper and cool completely on a wire rack.

6 Serve in slices spread with butter.

MAKING TIME 10–15 MINUTES
BAKING TIME 10 MINUTES

CLASSIC SPECIAL SCONES

The secret of a good scone is not to have the mixture too dry and not to handle the dough too much.

MAKES 10

- 2 cups (8 oz/225g) self-rising flour
- 1 level tsp baking powder
- 4 tbsp (2 oz/55g) butter
- 1 tablespoon (1 oz/25g) superfine sugar
- 1 large egg
- milk

1 Preheat the oven to 425°F/Convection 375°F and lightly grease a baking sheet.

2 Measure the flour and baking powder into a bowl, add the butter and rub in until the mixture resembles fine breadcrumbs. Stir in the sugar.

3 Crack the egg into a measuring jug, lightly beat then make up to ½ cup (4 oz/120ml) with the milk. Stir most of the egg and milk into the flour, keeping 1 tablespoon in the jug to glaze the scones before baking. Mix to a soft dough.

4 Turn on to a lightly floured surface, knead lightly, then roll out to ½ in thickness. Cut into rounds with a fluted 3 in cutter to make 10 scones.

5 Place the scones, well spaced, on the baking sheet. Brush the tops with the remaining egg and milk mixture and bake in the preheated oven for about 10 minutes, or until a pale golden brown.

6 Remove from the baking sheet and cool completely on a wire rack.

VARIATION: GOLDEN SCONES

Use light muscovado sugar instead of superfine and add 1 tablespoon of golden syrup to the milk and egg mixture. Beat thoroughly to blend before adding to the flour mixture.

MAKING TIME 10–15 MINUTES
BAKING TIME 10 MINUTES

WHOLEMEAL SCONES

The wholemeal flour makes a healthy addition—all the more reason to serve with clotted cream and jam!

MAKES 10

- 1 cup plus 1 tbsp (4½ oz/125g) self-rising flour
- 1 cup (4 oz/100g) whole-wheat flour
- 1 rounded tsp baking powder
- 4 tbsp (2 oz/55g) butter
- 1 tbsp (1 oz/25g) superfine sugar
- 1 large egg
- milk

1 Preheat the oven to 425°F/Convection 375°F and lightly grease a baking sheet.

2 Put the flours and baking powder in a bowl, add the butter and rub in until the mixture resembles fine breadcrumbs. Stir in the sugar.

3 Crack the egg into a measuring jug, lightly beat then make up to ½ cup (4 oz/120ml) with milk. Stir most of the egg and milk into the flour, keeping 1 tablespoon in the jug to glaze the scones before baking. Mix to a soft dough.

4 Turn on to a lightly floured surface, knead lightly, then roll out to ½ in thickness. Cut into rounds with a fluted 3 in cutter to make 10 scones.

5 Place the scones, well spaced, on the baking sheet. Brush the tops with the remaining egg and milk mixture and bake in the preheated oven for about 10 minutes, or until a pale golden brown.

6 Remove the scones from the baking sheet and cool completely on a wire rack.

VARIATION: FRUIT SCONES
Add ¼–⅓ cup (2–3 oz/50–75g) dried mixed fruit to the rubbed-in mixture.

MAKING TIME 10–15 MINUTES
BAKING TIME 10 MINUTES

CHEESE SCONES

Wrapping scones in a kitchen towel after baking helps to keep them moist.

MAKES 10

- 2 cups (8 oz/225g) self-rising flour
- 1 level tsp dry mustard
- ¼ level tsp salt
- good pinch of cayenne pepper
- 1 level tsp baking powder
- 4 tbsp (2 oz/55g) butter
- ½ cup (4 oz/100g) finely grated cheese
- 1 large egg
- milk

1 Preheat the oven to 425°F/Convection 375°F and lightly grease a baking sheet.

2 Measure the flour, mustard, salt, cayenne and baking powder into a bowl. Add the butter and rub in until the mixture resembles fine breadcrumbs. Stir in the cheese.

3 Crack the egg into a measuring jug, lightly beat it and then make up to ½ cup (4 oz/120ml) with milk. Stir most of the egg and milk into the flour, keeping 1 tablespoon in the jug to glaze the scones before baking. Mix to a soft dough.

4 Turn on to a lightly floured surface, knead lightly, then roll out to ½ in thickness. Cut into rounds with a fluted 3 in cutter to make 10 scones.

5 Place the scones, well spaced, on the baking sheet. Brush the tops with the remaining egg and milk mixture and bake in the preheated oven for about 10 minutes, or until a pale golden brown.

6 Remove from the oven and cool completely on a wire rack.

MAKING TIME 5 MINUTES
COOKING TIME 2–3 MINUTES

DROP SCONES

These are simple to make and a great standby when unexpected visitors pop in at the weekend.

MAKES 24

- 1¼ cups (6 oz/175g) self-rising flour
- 1 level tsp baking powder
- 2½ tbsp (1½ oz/40g) superfine sugar
- 1 large egg
- ¾ cup (6 oz/180ml) milk
- a little sunflower oil, to grease

1 Measure the flour, baking powder and sugar into a bowl. Make a well in the center, then add the egg and half the milk. Beat well with a whisk to a smooth, thick batter, then beat in enough milk to make the consistency of thick pouring cream.

2 Heat a large nonstick pan and grease with little oil.

3 Drop the mixture in teaspoonfuls on to the hot pan over a medium heat, spacing well apart to allow for them to spread. When bubbles appear on the surface, turn the scones over and cook on the other side for more, 30–60 seconds, or until lightly golden brown.

4 Lift the pancakes on to a wire rack and cover them with a clean kitchen towel to keep them soft.

5 Continue cooking until all the batter has been used, then serve warm with butter or blueberries and maple syrup.

VARIATION: MOLASSES DROP SCONES

Add 1 tablespoon of black molasses to the basic recipe and cut down the sugar to just 1 teaspoonful. For a change, add ¼ level teaspoon pumpkin pie spice to the flour.

MAKING TIME 5 MINUTES
COOKING TIME 2–3 MINUTES

CHEESE DROP SCONES

A lovely savory alternative to a sweet drop scone.

MAKES 24

- 1¼ cups (6 oz/175g) self-rising flour
- 1 level tsp baking powder
- ¼ cup (1 oz/30g) grated Parmesan
- ½ level tsp dry mustard
- ¼ level tsp salt
- 1 large egg
- ¾ cup (6 oz/180ml) milk
- a little sunflower oil, to grease

1 Measure the flour, baking powder, Parmesan, mustard and salt into a bowl. Make a well in the center, then add the egg and half the milk. Beat well with a whisk to a thick batter, then beat in enough milk to make the consistency of thick pouring cream.

2 Heat a large nonstick pan and grease with little oil.

3 Drop the mixture in teaspoonfuls on to the hot pan over a medium heat, spacing well apart to allow for them to spread. When bubbles appear on the surface, turn the scones over and cook on the other side for more, 30–60 seconds, or until lightly golden brown.

4 Lift the pancakes on to a wire rack and cover them with a clean kitchen towel to keep them soft.

5 Continue cooking until all the batter has been used then serve warm with butter.

MAKING TIME 10 MINUTES
COOKING TIME 6 MINUTES

WELSH CAKES

These are quick to make and may be made on a traditional griddle or in a heavy nonstick frying pan. The cakes are best eaten on the day that they are made.

MAKES 12–14

- 2 cups (8 oz/225g) self-rising flour
- ½ cup (4 oz/114g) butter
- ⅓ cup (3 oz/75g) superfine sugar, plus extra to dust
- ½ (3 oz/75g) currants
- ½ level tsp pumpkin pie spice
- 1 large egg
- 1 tbsp milk

1 Measure the flour into a bowl and rub in the butter until the mixture resembles fine breadcrumbs. Add the sugar, currants and spice.

2 Beat the egg with the milk and add this to the flour and currant mixture. Mix to a firm dough.

3 Roll out to ¼ in thickness and cut into rounds with a plain 3 in cutter.

4 Heat a griddle or heavy-based frying pan and grease lightly.

5 Cook the Welsh cakes over a low heat for about 3 minutes on each side until golden brown. Do not cook the cakes too fast otherwise the centers will not be cooked through.

6 Cool completely on a wire rack.

7 Dust with sugar and serve.

MAKING TIME 10 MINUTES
BAKING TIME 10 MINUTES

TRADITIONAL CHEESE STRAWS

Always popular with those who do not have a particularly sweet tooth, these are good to serve at a cocktail party.

MAKES 24

1¼ cups (7 oz/200g) self-rising flour
1 level tsp dry mustard
¼ level tsp salt
freshly ground black pepper
½ cup (4 oz/114g) butter
4½ oz (125g) mature Cheddar, grated
a little beaten egg

1 Preheat the oven to 400°F/Convection 350°F and lightly grease two or three baking sheets.

2 Measure the flour, mustard powder, salt and pepper into a bowl and rub in the butter until the mixture resembles fine breadcrumbs. Stir in the cheese, then add sufficient egg to give a firm dough. Turn out onto a lightly floured surface and knead until smooth.

3 Roll out to ¼ in thickness and cut into narrow strips.

4 Arrange on the baking sheets and bake in the preheated oven for about 10 minutes, or until just beginning to tinge with color.

5 Leave to cool on the sheets for a few moments, then lift off with an offset spatula and finish cooling on a wire rack.

MAKING TIME 15 MINUTES
PROVING TIME 1 HOUR
BAKING TIME 10–15 MINUTES

FAST GRANARY ROLLS

For lighter rolls, use half granary flour and half bread flour.

MAKES 24

- 1½ lb (675g) granary flour (available online)
- 1 × ¼ oz (7g) packet fast-acting yeast
- 2 level tsp sea salt, or a little less ordinary salt
- 1 tbsp sunflower oil
- 2 cups (16 oz/480ml) hand-hot milk, or milk and water mixed
- 1 large egg, beaten, to glaze

1 Grease two large baking sheets.

2 Put the plastic dough blade into the food processor, then add the dry ingredients and the oil. Process for a few seconds to mix them well, then add the liquid in a continuous stream through the feed-tube while the processor is on, to mix to a dough. Process for 2 minutes more in order to knead the dough.

3 Turn out onto a floured surface. Halve the dough and roll each half into a sausage shape. Divide each one into 12 equal pieces by cutting with a sharp knife. Shape the pieces into rounds by hand and place them, well spaced, onto the baking sheets.

4 Cover the rolls with plastic wrap and put the baking sheets into a warm place to proof for about 1 hour.

5 Preheat the oven to 425°F/Convection 375°F.

6 Once the rolls have doubled in size, glaze with the beaten egg and bake in the preheated oven for 10–15 minutes, or until they have browned on top and sound hollow when the base is tapped.

7 Cool on a wire rack.

MAKING TIME 10 MINUTES
BAKING TIME 35 MINUTES

IRISH SODA BREAD

If you run out of bread, this is a quick and easy recipe to make. It is best eaten fresh as a tea bread or as a substitute for yeast-baked bread. If you do not have soured milk, fresh milk may be soured by adding 1 tablespoon of lemon juice.

MAKES 1 LOAF

3⅓ cups (1 lb/450g) all-purpose flour
1 level tsp baking soda
1 level tsp salt
4 tbsp (2 oz/55g) butter
1¼ cups (10 oz/300ml) buttermilk or soured milk

1 Preheat the oven to 425°F/Convection 375°F and flour a baking sheet.

2 Sift the flour into a bowl with the baking soda and salt. Add the butter and rub in until it resembles breadcrumbs.

3 Make a well in the center and stir in the milk. Mix to a scone-like dough with a round-bladed knife.

4 Turn the dough onto a lightly floured surface and knead lightly. Shape into a 7 in round and then flatten slightly and place on a floured baking sheet.

5 Score the round with a knife twice, once lengthwise and once crosswise, and bake in the preheated oven for about 35 minutes, or until well risen and golden brown.

6 Cool completely on a wire rack then serve sliced, spread with butter.

BREAD

MAKING TIME 10 MINUTES
BAKING TIME 1 HOUR

CHEESE AND BRAZIL NUT LOAF

Make this loaf with whichever nuts you happen to have in your pantry. I particularly like it made with Brazil nuts.

MAKES 1 LOAF

- 1 cup (4 oz/100g) self-rising flour
- 1 cup (4 oz/100g) whole-wheat flour
- 1 level tsp baking powder
- 1 level tsp dry mustard
- 1 level tsp salt
- freshly ground black pepper
- 6 tbsp (3 oz/85g) butter, softened
- 4 oz (100g) extra mature Cheddar, grated
- ¼ cup (2 oz/50g) Brazil nuts, chopped
- 2 large eggs
- ½ cup (4 oz/120ml) milk

1 Preheat the oven to 350°F/Convection 320°F. Grease 8½ × 4½ (1 lb) loaf tin and line with nonstick baking paper.

2 Measure all the ingredients into a large mixing bowl and beat with an electric mixer until well blended.

3 Turn the mixture into the tin, level the top and bake in the preheated oven for about 1 hour, or until well risen. A skewer inserted into the center of the loaf should come out clean.

4 Leave to cool in the tin for about 5 minutes, then turn out and finish cooling on a wire rack.

INDEX

C

D

E

F

G

H

I

J

L

M

N

O

P

Q

R

S

T

V

W

Y

THANK YOUS

This book is a real team effort. Lucy Young has orchestrated the planning of it with her usual expertise and juggling skills!

Jo Roberts Miller, our lovely editor, has brought the book together with beautiful results. Jo is quite exceptional—never have we had an editor who has made so many of the recipes at home for her children! This is the seventh she has edited for us.

Lucinda McCord and Isla Murray have tested the recipes with great dedication. Baking can be tricky when testing recipes and they are the best at making sure the recipes are foolproof for everyone at home.

Muna Reyal, thank you for your idea of bringing this book back to life, and to the team at Headline Home for producing a brilliant book of which I am very proud.

Thank you to Emma and Alex Smith at Smith and Gilmour for the design, Georgia Glynn Smith for the creative photography, home economist Lisa Harrison for being the best and Felicity Bryan—my literary agent of over 40 years.

It has been a joy to bring this book right back up to date and thank you to my special team.